Candlelight Dinners

Julie Hamilton

Candlelight Dinners

Romantic meals for two

Macdonald

A Macdonald BOOK

© Julie Hamilton 1984

First published in Great Britain in 1984
by Macdonald & Co (Publishers) Ltd
London & Sydney

A member of BPCC plc

British Library Cataloguing in Publication Data

Hamilton, Julie
    Candlelight dinners.
    1. Cookery
    I. Title
    641.5'61   TX652

    ISBN 0-356-10453-2

Filmset by Flair Plan Photo-typesetting Limited

Printed and bound in Spain by
Printer Industria Gráfica SA, Barcelona. D.L.B. 27871-1984

Macdonald & Co (Publishers) Ltd
Maxwell House
74 Worship Street
London EC2A 2EN

The publishers wish to thank Mappin & Webb,
Regent Street, London, and The Design Council,
London, for the generous loan of some of the
tableware used in the photographs.

Photography by Rex Bamber

Stylist: Dawn Lane

Contents

Dedication

This book is for my youngest children – Esther, who was not very happy that I went away to write it but who is a most promising cook and a very special little person, and Damon, who bombarded me with letters to tell me how hungry he was and would I please hurry home! I really felt missed! I wrote this book in the Dordogne, France, in L'Ancienne Chapelle à Paunat, a charming house lent to me by Jancis Page, whom I wish to thank. Paunat offered a tranquility beyond description! There is one more important acknowledgement. I wish to thank the France Musique Radio Station for relaying, during my solitary stay in Paunat, a recording made in 1953 of Bruno Walter conducting the New York Philharmonic playing Mahler's Fourth Symphony at the Carnegie Hall with Ermgarde Seefried, soprano. It was one of the most moving and stimulating as well as interesting musical experiences I have ever had. France Musique kept me constantly supplied with a variety of music without which I certainly could not survive, let alone write.

Autumn 1983

Introduction

It is said that it was the morning after a delectable tête à tête dinner in Josephine's wood-panelled oval dining room in Rue Chantereine during the winter of 1795/6 that Napoleon Bonaparte penned the first of his famous and very remarkable love letters. 'I awaken full of you. Between your portrait and the memory of our intoxicating night my senses have no respite. Sweet and incomparable Josephine, what is this bizarre effect you have upon my heart?'

For as far back as anyone can recall food has played a spectacular part in almost every conceivable special occasion. We can communicate with food – we do business over a meal; we welcome dignitaries and royalty with a banquet. We also 'make love' with food – dinner by candlelight. It must be the most intensely pleasurable of tasks to prepare a dinner especially for someone with whom you are in love.

Every part of the preparations allows you to think of him, to turn over and over in your mind the forthcoming evening. The imagination rushes ahead, fantasizing on the compliments you will receive, the impression you will make, the pleasure you will be giving. A meal prepared with so much thought, attentiveness and love cannot be anything other than wonderful and revealing to the person for whom you have cooked it. Nothing could express more clearly what you feel for them, how much you care, or who you are!

For convenience I have laid out the candlelit recipes in individual menus. They are balanced to allow you not to spend too much time in the kitchen cooking after your guest arrives, although it is impossible to avoid a certain amount of last-minute preparation. Many of the best dishes call for quick, brief cooking and serving at once. The introduction to each menu will guide you as to whether and how much you can prepare in advance if you wish to.

Among the recipes I hope you will find a few you are familiar with as well as new dishes I have created for just such occasions that I have enjoyed. None of the dinners ask for skills beyond the ability of anyone cooking with love!

Now there is a paradoxical situation here – can you guess it? The last time I fell in love I lost my appetite; is it not often the case? Fortunately the candlelit dinner is not the prerogative of couples ecstatically and newly in love. It is also for the longstanding loving relationships, to toast a wedding anniversary, a birthday, or just for the joy of knowing someone. Such a dinner can say 'Hallo. Who are you?' or 'I like you' or 'Thank you for coming into my life'. Napoleon had a dinner that lasted just ten minutes in The Tuileries on 30 November 1809, to tell Josephine of his intention to divorce her. I don't think that can have been a very good meal so I will not provide a menu for such an occasion, which surely must be the appetite killer of all time! Besides,

cooking for 'goodbye' must certainly cause the custard to curdle, the mayonnaise to separate and the soufflé to flop! 'Hallo! I love you' is more to my liking.

My qualifications to write such a book as this are very straightforward – I love cooking, I have often fallen in love and cooked for him, and I still do! Fall in love or cook for him? you may ask. I married him. I have written about food for several years now but I have had no formal culinary training and my only real attributes are love and an insatiable urge to create, to talk with food and to express myself through food.

I am not greatly in favour of short cuts and I prefer using fresh ingredients whenever possible. Everyday cooking for the family is a different matter; short cuts and convenience foods can of course be used from time to time, but meals as special as the ones proposed in this book should be prepared with the vital ingredients, care and love, patience and time, and should be presented with style.

A word of warning. Remember, before you choose your menu, to be sure you know whether the person you are cooking for likes his meat in general well done or rare. Or perhaps he is allergic to shellfish. Dinner for two can be very embarrassing if your guest has to leave half the meal; it is quite impossible for it to go unnoticed.

Candles and flowers, winter twigs and polished apples, white napkins and sparkling glasses all show style and help to create a special atmosphere, but nothing says more than the obvious evidence of the loving trouble you have taken.

The human frame being what it is, heart, body and brain all mixed up together, and not contained in separate compartments as they will be no doubt in another million years, a good dinner is of great importance to good talk. One cannot think well, love well, sleep well, if one has not dined well.

A Room of One's Own by Virginia Woolf

An Intimate Evening

Crudités served with a Garlic Mayonnaise

Breast of Pheasant
Tagliatelle Verdi
Tomato Salad

Apricot and Lime Chantilly

At least half of this meal could be prepared in advance without detriment to it. Your last-minute work will involve the grilling of the prepared pheasant breasts and cooking the tagliatelle. I would recommend doing the final cooking just before sitting at table, but the main dish should be assembled at the very last moment.

Crudités can consist of any fresh raw vegetable you like, the wider the choice the better. The mayonnaise could be an aioli, but I think it would not be very tactful to serve it on such an occasion unless you are absolutely certain of your partner's taste!

As only the breast of the pheasant is used you will have the rest of the bird left over, and I suggest you make either a terrine or game soup with it for later consumption. A terrine (see page 87) would keep in the fridge for at least a month, and game soup can be frozen.

The Chantilly could easily be made the day before, in fact it is probably better if it is.

Crudités with Garlic Mayonnaise

It is a good idea to make the mayonnaise well in advance, but the simple preparation of the vegetables and their decorative arrangement on the dish should be done as late as possible to avoid the tired look they are apt to acquire so easily.

1 or 2 cloves of garlic
1 pinch each of sugar, salt and
pepper
1 scant teaspoon Dijon mustard
1 or 2 egg yolks or 1 egg (see method)
approx. ¼ pint/150 ml best olive oil
2 or 3 teaspoons lemon juice
suggested vegetables: carrot, fennel
cut in thin strips, cauliflower
broken into florets, celery,
cucumber cut into strips, very
fresh closed mushrooms, very
young courgettes slit lengthwise.
Do not include tomatoes, as you
will be serving them later.

There are two ways of making this mayonnaise, the purist's way and the fool-proof food-processor way. Purist's first. Using a pestle and mortar pound and crush the garlic with the salt and sugar until it is quite liquid, add the mustard and pepper and one or two egg yolks. Use two if your cloves of garlic are large ones. With a wooden spoon beat the ingredients thoroughly and vigorously. When well blended begin to add the olive oil while still beating, a drop at a time (really a drop only to begin with) then as the mayonnaise begins to thicken you can add the oil in a fine thin stream, but be careful – if you go too fast it will separate. When you have used two thirds of the oil add a little lemon juice, then continue with the oil. Finish off with lemon to taste and adjust seasoning. If the consistency is too thin add more olive oil.

Should mayonnaise happen to separate, all is not lost. Simply beat another egg yolk in a clean bowl and very, very slowly add the curdled mixture to it.

Fool proof method. Use the whole of just one egg for this method. Put all the ingredients except the oil in the processor and process until everything is well blended. Then, with the machine still switched on, add the oil in a steady stream. Adjust consistency by adding more oil or lemon.

It is rather attractive to serve

the mayonnaise in the mortar if you have used one, otherwise turn it out into a suitable pot, cover and keep in a coolish place until needed. To serve, place the pot of mayonnaise in the centre of a large plate and arrange the crudités decoratively round it. Some cubes of ice dotted about the vegetables will help to keep them crisp and fresh. This dish is best eaten with fingers.

Breast of Pheasant

The size of the bird and appetites will determine whether you need one or two pheasants. Personally I would look for a plump henbird and offer only one breast if I have planned to serve the first course and dessert. Not too much of something very delicious can only result in the hope of being asked again to eat at your table, the ultimate compliment!

1 large hen pheasant, plucked, drawn and well hung
2 teaspoons dried mushrooms
1 tablespoon white wine
1 oz/25 g butter

2 thick rashers of fatty bacon
juice of ½ small lemon with ½ teaspoon honey dissolved in it (gentle heat will dissolve the honey)
½ teaspoon finely chopped fresh thyme
¼ teaspoon whole-grain mustard
4 tablespoons single cream

If you are in doubt about removing the breast from the bird and keeping it intact then ask your butcher to do it for you. Any butcher worth his salt enjoys displaying the skills so rarely asked for these days when supermarket shopping seems to have taken over.

Place each portion of breast separately between greaseproof paper and bash gently with a small heavy saucepan to flatten them slightly. Cut 2 pieces of foil double the size of each portion. Soak the dried mushrooms in the wine to rehydrate them. Melt the butter in a frying pan and fry the breasts (separately if your pan is small) for 2 or 3 minutes, turning them frequently. Place them on the foil. Chop the bacon very finely and put it on top of each breast. Dribble the

lemon and honey over, season with plenty of pepper and then sprinkle with thyme. Fold the foil over to make 2 tightly sealed parcels. Tip the wine and mushrooms into the frying pan from which you have removed the breasts, stir well to deglaze and add the mustard and cream, bring to simmering point and cook until reduced and slightly thickened.

The final stage of this dish should be done at the last possible moment. Heat the grill, place the parcels under it, and, turning them frequently, cook for about 6 minutes, then open the foil and allow the bacon to brown and crispen a little. Remove from the foil, place on a hot serving dish and pour the sauce round each breast.

Tagliatelle Verdi

To cook the pasta, use a large saucepan and boil plenty of salted water fast for a minute or two before adding it. Test by tasting to see if it is cooked; do not go by the instructions on the packet, which are often misleading because they do not take into account the degree of freshness of the pasta. Dress the cooked tagliatelle with a little oil or butter according to taste and serve it in a very hot dish.

Tomato Salad

The success of a tomato salad lies in the quality of the tomatoes and olive oil used. I do not favour raw onions in this salad, and I do not think they are particularly romantic!

2 large Dutch beef tomatoes or 4
  smaller ones
freshly chopped marjoram (or dried
  oregano) to taste
salt and lots of pepper
just a few drops of wine vinegar
1 tablespoon best olive oil

Peel the tomatoes unless you are certain the skins are tender (this is easily done if you plunge them in and out of boiling water). Cut them into small chunks, sprinkle the other ingredients over them, and mix lightly. Nothing more is needed when the tomatoes are really good and the salad accompanies a highly flavoured main course. Do not refrigerate; serve at room temperature.

Apricot and Lime Chantilly

½ lime
5 oz/150 g dried apricots
1 oz/25 g sugar
1 tablespoon apricot or plum brandy
  (or similar liqueur)
2 tablespoons cream, whipped
1 dessertspoon toasted flaked
  almonds

Shred the half lime as finely as possible, skin and pulp together. Wash the apricots. Place both together in a saucepan and just cover with water. Bring to simmering point and cook for about 20 minutes, then add the sugar, stir and cook very slowly until most of the liquid has been absorbed by the apricots. Test that they are cooked through; if not add a little more water and continue to cook. Cool and push through a sieve or the finest disc of a vegetable mouli. Flavour the purée with the apricot brandy, stir in the whipped cream and toasted flaked almonds. Turn into individual little pots or soufflé dishes and chill until needed.

A Simple Extravagance

Scallops Brochettes
(Scallops grilled on Skewers)

Lamb Guard of Honour
New Potatoes
Sweet and Spiced Onions and Carrots

Stem Ginger Ice Cream

This menu has a simplicity that should be appealing; it is quite easy to prepare and yet appears extravagant. Apart from the ice cream, it is not possible to do more in advance than prepare the food for cooking and set the table. But as all the food is simple to cook, and doesn't require much attention from you while it is cooking, you will find that you can do it without your guest even realizing that your attention is divided between him (or her) and the kitchen!

Scallops Brochettes

The season for scallops is autumn to early spring, but frozen scallops are now readily available in most fishmongers.

6 scallops
1 clove of garlic
4 rashers of bacon
salt and pepper
a pinch of herbes de provence
oil
lemon juice
2 crisp cos lettuce leaves or chicory if
  you cannot find cos

If the scallops are fresh the fishmonger will probably have opened and prepared them for you; this should be done in front of you to ensure their freshness. If you buy them fresh and closed in their shells, simply open them and remove the flesh and coral, wash them in several changes of water then dry them gently with kitchen paper. If they are large scallops cut them in half. Rub the skewers with the clove of garlic, then discard it. Cut the bacon into squares. Thread the scallops, their corals and the bacon alternately on the skewers. Season generously with salt, pepper and the herbs. Dribble the oil over each brochette and place under a hot grill. Cook, turning from time to time, for about 10 to 12 minutes. Serve sprinkled with lemon juice on the cos lettuce leaf. A finger or two of brown toast would go well.

Lamb Guard of Honour

This is just a fancy way of presenting best end of lamb. You will need to ask your butcher to prepare a guard of honour especially for you, stating that it is only for two people and therefore you will only want four chops, or six if they are small enough. Make sure the butcher gives you the trimmings. It is a matter of taste whether you like lamb well done or pink. Long slow cooking tends to bring out the full and strong flavour of lamb; eaten pink it is more delicate.

1 Guard of Honour

For the stuffing
1 apple, cooking or dessert
2 or 3 good sprigs of fresh mint (or,
  if out of season, 1 dessertspoon
  strong mint sauce)
the lamb trimmings very finely
  minced
2 tablespoons fresh breadcrumbs
1 egg
1 teaspoon sugar
½ teaspoon salt
a generous grating of nutmeg
small quantity flour

Prepare the following stuffing well in advance. Peel, core and finely grate the apple, mix it with the mint finely chopped and combine with the sugar, minced lamb trimmings and breadcrumbs. Add the seasoning and the egg, well beaten. Work all the ingredients well together and stuff the cavity of the lamb. Any remaining stuffing can be rolled into balls, dusted with flour and cooked round the joint. Cover the ends of the

Love Italian Style

bones with foil to prevent them burning. Dust the joint all over with seasoned flour and roast in a pre-heated oven at 350°F/ 180°C/Gas Mark 4 for 25 minutes to the pound (weighed after stuffing), plus a further 25 minutes at 300°F/150°C/Gas Mark 2.

New Potatoes

These can be cooked in the oven too. You need about 5 each depending on size. Simply wash them, leaving their skins on, put them on a bed of mint or thyme in an ovenproof earthenware pot, sprinkle with salt, a little lemon juice and a spoonful of oil, put the lid on and cook in the lower part of the oven while the meat is cooking.

Happy Anniversary

Sweet and Spiced Carrots and Onions

You need very small onions, or shallots if you like. Spring onions would do too; they should be no bigger than cherries.

2 medium to large carrots
10 baby onions
1 oz/25 g butter
1 teaspoon oil
a generous pinch of the following:
  allspice, cinnamon, crushed
  coriander and freshly grated
  ginger
1 teaspoon wine vinegar
salt, pepper and sugar to taste

Slice the carrots into thin strips. Peel the onions until they reach the size of cherries, or if they are spring onions simply trim them. Combine all the ingredients in a flameproof earthenware dish and cook very gently over a low heat, stirring from time to time, until cooked to your taste (which for me is with plenty of bite).

Stem Ginger Ice Cream

Some people hate ginger, so beware! The quantities given here will make considerably more than two people can eat but it is not worth making it in too small a quantity. Of course, it keeps well if you have a freezer, although you do not need one to make it with; the freezing compartment of the fridge will do. If you have an electric ice-cream maker so much the better, if not follow these instructions; you will need time to complete the task.

4 oz/100 g stem ginger preserved in
  vinegar
½ pint/300 ml double or whipping
  cream
4 eggs (3 whole plus one yolk only)
2 tablespoons caster sugar
2 fl oz/3 tablespoons ginger wine

Strain the ginger and pound it to a smooth paste. Combine it with all the other ingredients. Pour the mixture into a bain-marie and thicken, stirring continuously over not quite boiling water. Strain and allow to cool before attempting to freeze, either according to the instructions on your ice-cream maker or as follows. Turn up the freezer or the freezing compartment of your fridge to the highest number, which should be the lowest temperature. Tip the ice-cream mixture into a chilled container and place in the freezer. Whisk with a fork or balloon whisk every 30 minutes until the cream is half frozen. At that stage remove it to a chilled bowl and thoroughly beat it with an electric whisk, then return it to the freezer until fully frozen.

To serve, remove from freezer and place in fridge before you sit down to the table. It should then have reached the right consistency to enable you to scoop out attractive portions when you are ready. Langues de chat are much nicer than wafers to serve with homemade ice cream. Also, a little chocolate melted and poured over each portion can be a delicious addition.

Part of the art of successful entertaining is the setting of the scene. The lighting, the colour of the dinner service, the extra attention given to the laying of the table and the flowers are almost as important as the food. One beautiful bloom floating in a brandy balloon half filled with water can be quite stunning and transform the simplest of tables into a simple extravagance.

Love Italian Style

Spaghetti with Seafood Sauce

*Veal Escalopes cooked in Sage, Lemon and Butter
served with Broccoli Spears*

*Fresh Raspberries or Strawberries
marinated and served in White Wine*

This menu is very Italian in style; the meat with only one vegetable is a lighter course than the first one, which is not at all unusual in Italy. The fruit dessert is served in wine without cream and is quite delicious. I have suggested using white wine but they often use red wine in Italy so it is up to you to choose what is most convenient or perhaps the wine you think would go with the chosen fruit – and it does not need to be a sweet one. My favourite with fruit is a light dry Italian rosé. The seafood sauce may be prepared in advance and reheated. You can even cook the spaghetti beforehand and leave it in cold water with a spoon of oil added, then drain and simply plunge it into fast boiling water for a couple of seconds before serving.

Spaghetti with Seafood Sauce

The fish you put in this sauce can vary depending on availability and taste. Almost any combination works providing you make absolutely certain you have removed every bone. It once happened that I was entertaining to dinner a singer, an Italian baritone, and I served a fish dish which called for boned fish. One bone escaped my notice and ended in the throat of my singer. That was the end of any romance there might have been that evening! So take great care.

3 or 4 cloves of garlic
3 tablespoons of olive oil
1 14 oz (396 g) can tomatoes
a large bunch of parsley
10 whitebait
1 or 2 squid tubes if available
4 oz/100 g white fish such as hus (dog or catfish) or monk fish
2 oz/50 g cod or haddock
2 sardines (fresh, not canned)
3 or 4 anchovy fillets
6 king size prawns
2 oz/50 g mussels
2 oz/50 g cockles or clams
2 tablespoons red wine vinegar or red wine
plenty of pepper
6 oz/175 g spaghetti

Coarsely chop the garlic and, in a heavy bottomed saucepan, brown it in the oil. Put the tomatoes through the fine disc of a vegetable mouli to remove the seeds and add them to the garlic. Scissor the parsley into the tomatoes, simmer while you prepare the fish. Clean and remove all trace of bones and cut into bite-sized pieces, leaving the whitebait whole, of course, as their bones are harmless. Do not peel the prawns (but be sure to lay a good-size finger bowl and napkins when you set the table). Add all the fish except the cockles, clams, mussels and prawns to the tomato sauce. Add the wine vinegar, bring to simmering point and cook uncovered for 10 minutes, then add the remaining items. Remove from flame but keep very hot until you are ready to serve, or if you have made this in advance, allow it to cool and reheat when needed.

To serve, cook the spaghetti in plenty of fast-boiling water, heat a serving bowl and tip the hot sauce into it, mix in the cooked spaghetti and season with pepper. Be sure to heat the plates thoroughly too.

Veal Escalopes in Sage, Lemon and Butter with Broccoli Spears

This must be the quickest and easiest dish to present at a table for two. You can either cook the meat, which only takes a few minutes, when you have finished your first course or just before you sit down and keep it hot.

3 oz/75 g unsalted butter
2 or 3 leaves of fresh sage (a pinch of dried would just about do)
2 veal escalopes approx. 4 or 5 oz/100 or 150 g, which you or your butcher have beaten out so they are almost wafer thin
a little flour
seasoning
8 oz/225 g broccoli, or more if liked
1 tablespoon fresh lemon juice

Melt half the butter in a large heavy bottomed frying pan, scissor in the sage. Dust the veal escalopes with well-seasoned flour and fry, turning several times, over a fairly fierce heat until pale gold. Remove to a large hot serving dish and surround with the broccoli spears which have simply been plunged into salted boiling water and cooked uncovered for barely 5 minutes. Pour the lemon juice into the frying pan, stir to deglaze, then add the remaining butter. Pull off the heat and stir vigorously until the butter is melted, then pour all over the meat and broccoli.

Note: Serve at once, and remember to warm the plates thoroughly. The attractive appearance of this dish is more easily achieved if you have trimmed the broccoli to equal lengths before cooking.

Raspberries or Strawberries in White Wine

No exact quantities need be given here, just a little advice. First of all do not at any stage put the fruit in the fridge after you have prepared it. It must be served at room temperature. The less handling soft fruit has the better, so it is best to portion it out into individual bowls immediately. Pour over it enough wine to come barely half way up the fruit, and sprinkle a little brown sugar on top. Mix gently and leave to stand for 1 hour if possible. A dash of Angostura bitters would add something mysterious and delightful to the flavour, and a single small flower or a fresh young sprig of mint or rosemary placed in the dish with the raspberries or strawberries will make them look extra special.

A Game Affair

Courgettes baked with Tomatoes and Anchovies

Partridge à la Normande
Sauté Potatoes
French Beans
Mushroom Salad — optional

Crème renversée au Choix Surprise

This menu depends on certain things being in season, although seasons will matter less and less as marketing progresses. Game birds are already being farmed, as well as being available frozen, and we will soon be able to buy them whenever we want. Somehow that makes them less special, less romantic; it's that age-old principle of 'the hard-to-get' being the most desirable. And that does not only apply to food, does it?

But hard- or easy-to-get, partridge cooked this way is marvellously special and should be regarded as a rare treat.

Courgettes Baked with Tomatoes and Anchovies

This dish may be served cold if you like, and providing you have not overcooked it you can even eat it with fingers as an accompaniment to pre-dinner drinks. In my opinion, like so many vegetable dishes that owe their creation to earlier origins in the Mediterranean countries, this dish is at its best served tepid. It can be made in advance without any worry.

2 medium-sized courgettes
2 tablespoons olive oil
4 cloves of garlic
1 14 oz (396 g) can of tomatoes
fresh (or dried) basil or marjoram
salt and pepper
4 anchovy fillets

Slice the courgettes in half lengthways, use a teaspoon to scoop out the pulp that contains the seeds. Sprinkle a little salt over them and leave to stand while you prepare the tomato sauce. Heat the oil in a heavy based pan and colour the whole peeled cloves of garlic.

Push the tomatoes through the fine disc of a mouli and add them to the garlic. Bring to simmering point and cook uncovered until reduced considerably, at least by one half, then add the herb and season to taste. Rinse and pat dry the courgettes; lightly oil a gratin dish, place them in it, fill each one with the tomato sauce and lay an anchovy fillet on top. Bake in a preheated oven at 375 or 400°F/190 or 200°C/Gas Mark 5 or 6 for approximately 20 minutes, until the courgettes are soft but not mushy. It is better to under than overcook.

Partridge à la Normande

It is usual when roasting or grilling partridge to serve one per person; whether you choose to will depend upon your appetites. If in any doubt allow one each.

This dish can be prepared well in advance up to the stage of putting it in the oven. It takes about 45 minutes to 1 hour to cook, and you serve it straight from the casserole, so there is not too much to do at the last minute.

4 or 6 medium-size cooking apples
3 oz/75 g butter
2 small partridges, trussed
1 tablespoon Calvados
2 tablespoons cream
seasoning

Peel and slice the apples not too thinly, toss them in half the butter to coat them thoroughly. Line the bottom of an earthenware casserole with some, and set the rest aside.

Heat the remaining butter in a frying pan and using a fierce heat, brown the partridges quickly all over. Place them on top of the apples in the casserole and surround them with the remaining apples. Deglaze the frying pan with calvados, having first pulled it off the heat, and pour it over the partridges. Season with salt and pepper and pour the cream over. Cover and cook in a preheated hot oven 400°F/200°C/Gas Mark 5 for approximately 45 minutes. Bring to table in the casserole.

The Vegetables

Sauté potatoes are perfect when entertaining, being one of the few vegetable dishes that really reheat well. Boil the potatoes in their skins; when cool enough to handle peel them and cut into chunks. Heat a mixture of oil and butter in a large heavy based pan and sauté the potatoes, seasoned with a little allspice and salt. Transfer them to a heated serving dish only at the very last minute.

The French beans, in my view, are well dressed in lemon and a few drops of high-quality olive oil, then served tepid, but that is a matter of taste. The only rule it is important to adhere to is not to overcook any vegetable; all are better slightly undercooked – with the possible exception of the potato.

Mushroom Salad

1 clove of garlic, finely chopped
¼ teaspoon French mustard
1 tablespoon olive oil
1 dessertspoon white wine vinegar
¾ teaspoon salt
pinch of sugar
6 closed very fresh white mushrooms
1 head of chicory

Make a vinaigrette dressing by combining the garlic, the mustard, the olive oil, the vinegar and the sugar and seasoning, in the bowl in which the salad is to be served. Slice the mushrooms and the chicory evenly about ¼ inch/5 mm thick and mix them together in the dressing just before serving.

Crème renversée au Choix Surprise

This is simply an attractive name for a delicious inverted cream custard – the 'choix surprise' being whatever liqueur you happen to have handy to flavour it with.

2 whole eggs plus 2 yolks
2 oz/50 g caster sugar
7 fl. oz/200 ml single cream
1½ tablespoons of liqueur

Scald the cream with the liqueur in it. Beat the eggs together with the sugar until very pale and light, and add the cream, stiring constantly until the mixture is well combined. Strain into a buttered ovenproof mould or oval dish (remembering you have to turn out the cooked cream), place it in a pan of hot water and bake at 325°F/160°C/Gas Mark 3 for approximately 30 minutes. To test if it is done insert a knife in the centre – it should come out clean. Cool the custard; when cold loosen carefully round the edges with a knife and invert on to a serving dish.

Happy Anniversary

Avocado Stuffed with Chilli Hot Crab

Roast Duckling with Plum and Brandy Sauce
Brussels Sprouts with Hazelnuts
Creamed Potatoes

Pecan and Honey Pie

This is a fairly rich meal, very suitable for a cosy evening by an open fire on a cold winter's night. Having said that, I must also add that I have cooked this meal in the middle of the summer with equal success! Very little last-minute attention is needed. The avocado takes only seconds to prepare, especially if you have mixed the crab filling in advance. The pecan and honey pie must be made well ahead of time as it needs to chill for an hour. So to the duck. Well, cooking duck is easy, you roast it and that's that. The sauce and vegetables require some attention, of course, but altogether this is a far simpler meal to produce than the menu could lead you to believe.

Avocado Stuffed with Chilli Hot Crab

1 fresh red chilli
½ red pepper (capsicum)
2 teaspoons oil
1 teaspoon tomato purée
1 teaspoon wine vinegar
2 tablespoons (heaped) of crab meat
  (this could be fresh or canned)
1 large or 2 small avocados
salt and pepper
a little butter

Slice the chilli open lengthways and scrape out the seeds. Cut the red pepper into three or four pieces, removing the seeds. Heat the oil and soften the chilli and pepper in it. When cooked, push it through a fine sieve and return it to the pan, add the tomato purée, vinegar and crab meat, stir to heat through and thoroughly combine. Taste, and adjust the seasoning if necessary. Just before sitting down to dinner, heat the grill, slice the avocados in half lengthways and remove the stone. Pile the stuffing into the cavity, brush the exposed flesh with softened butter and place under the grill for a couple of minutes at the most. A warmed slice of Greek pitta bread would go well.

Roast Duckling with Plum and Brandy Sauce

When buying the duckling choose the smallest you can find. Ask your butcher to cut it in half then truss it together again as a whole. If it is not possible to get the butcher to do this then you can do it yourself; the use of poultry shears will make it quite easy. Of course, it is not essential to do this. Cutting the bird in half before cooking it is simply to make it easy to serve – you just cut the string. However, if your duck is a largish one, it would perhaps be wise to leave it whole, as the half duck might look too big and clumsy on the plate.

1 small duckling

For the Sauce
6 oz/175 g stoned red plums (you could use canned ones)
¼ pint/150 ml demi-glace sauce
(reduced dark brown stock seasoned and usually made from veal, but could be imitated here by reducing and seasoning canned consommé)
a few drops of Worcestershire sauce
1 scant teaspoon soy sauce
1 tablespoon brandy

Make this simple sauce ahead of time and reheat at the last minute. If using fresh plums, stew them, sweetened to taste, until they disintegrate, and combine them with all the other ingredients. What could be simpler? Just pour the bubbling hot sauce over the duck as you serve it. Roasting duck is very easy, it is just a matter of deciding whether you favour long slow cooking or fast and fierce. I have used both methods with equal success, so perhaps you should be guided by the time available.

Fierce method: rub salt into the skin of the duckling and cover the breast with a piece of buttered foil. Preheat the oven to 425°F/220°C/Gas Mark 7. Put the duckling on a rack in a roasting tin and cook for 15 minutes to the pound plus 15 or 20 minutes extra at the end with the foil removed.

Slow method: preheat oven to 325°F/160°C/Gas Mark 3. Rub salt over the duck and cook uncovered for 1 hour, then remove from the oven, dust lightly with seasoned flour (a little cinnamon in it is nice) and cook for a further 25 to 45 minutes depending on size of duck.

Brussels Sprouts with Hazelnuts

The quantity of sprouts is a matter of judgment depending on size. I tend to think in terms of about ten per person, unless they are very big ones.

2 oz/50 g shelled and coarsely chopped hazelnuts
1 oz/25 g butter
about 20 sprouts
1 teaspoon lemon juice

Fry the hazelnuts in the butter and keep warm. Cook the sprouts in fast-boiling salted water. Drain off the water, toss them in the lemon juice and put in a hot serving dish. Tip the hazelnuts on top.

Creamed Potatoes

I think the best creamed potatoes are made by first boiling them in their skins in plenty of water, then, while still hot, peeling them and pushing them through the finest disc of a mouli. Add butter, cream and seasoning and whisk with a fork. Place the creamed potatoes in a buttered ovenproof dish, sprinkle the top with nutmeg and set aside until needed. Reheat in the oven until the top begins to colour lightly.

Do not be temped to use a food processor or blender to make creamed potatoes; the end result usually resembles a thick, gluey paste and for some reason tastes rather like one! In other words, there is no shortcut to success here.

Pecan and Honey Pie

This is a really delicious rich and gorgeous dessert – it is a sort of 'forbidden food' which makes it taste even better. These quantities will make a pie somewhat larger than you really need for two people, but it is one of those recipes which become awkward when the amounts are, say, halved. As it keeps well, I have not tried to reduce the size for two portions. This will serve four generously. Or it could allow for the outrageous to happen – a second helping!

For the pastry (pâte sablée)
4 oz/100 g plain flour
1 oz/25 g caster sugar
grated rind of ¼ lemon
1 oz/25 g ground almonds
3 oz/75 g butter
1 egg yolk
1 dessertspoon dark cane rum

For the filling
6 oz/175 g sugar
3 tablespoons water
7 oz/200 g pecan nuts, roughly chopped
1 tablespoon clear honey
¼ pint/150 ml whipped double cream

Mix together the flour, sugar, lemon rind and ground almonds. Work the butter in with your fingers. Combine the egg and rum. Make a well in the middle and tip the egg and rum into it. Using your fingers, pull the flour mixture into the liquid and work to a smooth paste as fast as possible, form into a ball, wrap it in greased foil and chill for 30 minutes.

Grease an 8-inch/20-centimetre flan tin and line it with the pâte sablée. Bake blind (as described on page 83) until pale golden, in a preheated oven 325°F/160°C/Gas Mark 3 (approximately 20 minutes).

To make the filling, melt the sugar in the water over a gentle heat and cook it until it caramelizes; remove it from the heat and add the pecan nuts and honey. Mix well and turn into a bowl to cool. When cold, thoroughly fold in the whipped cream, spread this filling in the now cooled flan case and chill for 1 hour before serving.

I have often made this pie a day before it was needed and found it even better as a result. The freshness of the pecan nuts is important, so if in any doubt, toss them over a fierce heat in a dry frying pan for a few minutes.

From Russia with Love

King Size Prawns on a Skewer

Beef Stroganoff served with
Rice and Peas
Green Salad

Apricot and Cinnamon Tartelettes

Not very much of this menu can be prepared in advance, except of course the tartelettes. On the other hand, it does not take very long to cook it. There are several versions of beef stroganoff but the one I give here is, in my view, the best and most resembles the dish as I had it in Russia. It requires the best fillet steak and should be cooked right at the very last moment, served straight from pan to plate. Please do not be tempted to economize and use rump or any other cut of steak then fillet; the end result would let you down because it simply would not be as good.

A glass of ice-cold vodka with the first course would not only be an excellent complement to the prawns, but also most appropriate to the theme of this meal.

King Size Prawns on a Skewer

12 prawns
1 oz/25 g butter
·2 teaspoons lemon juice
salt and pepper
parsley for garnish

Thread the prawns, without peeling them, onto the skewers. Melt the butter and mix the lemon with it. Season with salt and plenty of pepper and brush it over the skewered prawns. Place them under a very hot grill and heat them through while turning frequently. Serve at once with more butter and lemon painted over them and garnished with deep-fried parsley. Serve with finger bowls and napkins.

Beef Stroganoff served with Rice and Peas

12 oz/350 g fillet steak (more if you
*   like)*
1 oz/25 g butter
1 dessertspoon finely grated onion
2 oz/50 g small closed white
*   mushrooms, thinly sliced*
5 fl oz/150 ml sour cream
salt, pepper and allspice

Trim the fillet steak so there is not one speck of fat or sinew on it. Cutting across the grain, slice the steak into thin strips a little over $\frac{1}{4}$ inch (5 millimetres) wide. Melt the butter and toss the onion in it, add the steak and mushrooms, stir briskly over a fierce heat for barely 1 minute then mix in the sour cream and seasoning. Bring to boiling point and serve. If you like a sharper flavour include a little French mustard.

Serve with buttered rice and peas mixed together. This could have been cooked earlier and reheated over boiling water if need be.

Green Salad

Serve a simple green salad dressed by sprinkling sugar, lemon juice, dill weed, salt and a little oil in that order and then tossing.

What lettuce is available depends on the time of year. My favourite is the extraordinarily expensive iceberg, which seems to be in season most of the year. Its crispness and flavour are unsurpassable in my view. Nevertheless, a very delicious green salad can be made from fresh Chinese leaves mixed with watercress, and just the hearts of the common cabbage lettuce, when in season, are hard to beat.

Apricot and Cinnamon Tartelettes

A very versatile and easy dessert. You can fill the individual pastry cases with anything you like really – even strawberries sitting on whipped cream.

For the pastry (pâte sucrée)
4 oz/100 g plain flour
2 oz/50 g butter
2 egg yolks
2 oz/50 g caster sugar

For the filling
1 oz/25 g unsalted butter
1 oz/25 g icing sugar
½ teaspoon cinnamon
4 oz/100 g double cream cheese
1 tablespoon thick double cream
8 canned apricot halves or fresh ones
  stoned and stewed
1 egg white lightly beaten
caster sugar for dredging

To make the pastry, sift the flour into a pile on a flat surface, make a well in the middle and put in the soft butter, egg yolks and sugar, work them together with your fingers and pull in the flour. Mix and knead quickly until smooth. Wrap in foil or a plastic bag and chill for 1 hour. Roll out, line small individual tartlet tins and bake blind for approximately 10 minutes, until only pale gold, in a preheated oven 375°F/190°C/Gas Mark 5. The flavour will not be very good if you allow them to go a deeper colour.

For the filling, combine the butter, sifted sugar, cinnamon and cream cheese. Fold in the thick cream (if it's not really thick, whip it a little) and fill each pastry case with this mixture. Cut the apricot halves into crescent-shaped slices and arrange in an overlapping circle on top of the cream mixture. Brush with the lightly beaten egg white and dredge with caster sugar. Leave at room temperature. I do not recommend preparing these tartelettes too far ahead, as the pastry, once filled, will lose its crispness after a while.

A word about the apricots; if you can find fresh ripe ones that do not need to be cooked, you will have the very best. Then it is important to slice them as thinly as possible. The slight tartness of the raw fruit is really delicious with the sweet pastry and cream cheese filling, so it is well worth the extra hunting for ripe eating apricots.

Roman Holiday

Sardines Marinated with Fresh Mint

Veal and Sage Baked on Skewers
Mandorlata di Peperoni
Pasta Shells Tossed in Butter

Kiwi Fruit with Stem Ginger and Lemon

This menu is for lovers of Italy and Italian food. With the exception of the dessert, this menu is almost authentic and you could expect to eat such a meal probably anywhere in Italy, so maybe you will evoke memories of a blissful summer holiday in Italy and re-create a little of that mood with this dinner; or maybe it will whet the appetite and suggest further excursions in that direction.

Although the dessert has nothing whatsoever to do with Italy, its flavour is a delightful complement to the main course and a refreshing way to end the meal.

Opposite: *Roman Holiday*   Overleaf left: *A Way to a Man's Heart*   Overleaf right: *Easy Does It*

Sardines Marinated with Fresh Mint

This should be prepared two days in advance. It does not really matter what kind of fish you use so long as they are fairly small.

6 sardines
flour to coat them
oil to fry them in
1 scant teaspoon salt
3 tablespoons olive oil
1 large clove of garlic
1 tablespoon chopped fresh mint plus
    1 whole sprig
4 tablespoons wine vinegar
1 teaspoon sugar

Bone the fish unless they are very small. Wash and pat dry. Dust with flour and deep fry until well browned, drain and pat off surplus fat with kitchen paper. Arrange the fish decoratively in an earthenware or pottery dish. Sprinkle the salt over.

Heat the oil, add the garlic and chopped mint, fry gently until the garlic colours, then add the vinegar, the sugar and a pinch of pepper. Simmer for 3 minutes or so. Lay the whole sprig of mint on top of the fish and strain the marinade over it. Serve cold, preferably after resting for not less than 2 days.

Veal and Sage Baked on Skewers

Fresh sage is essential to this recipe. It is possible to prepare the meat ready for cooking in advance so all you have to do is pop the skewers of meat into the oven.

12 oz/350 g lean veal (not cut thin
    as for escalopes)
8 thick slices of wholemeal bread
4 fresh sage leaves
3 oz/75 g butter
salt and plenty of pepper

Cut the veal into regular-sized cubes about 1½ inches (4 centimetres) square. Remove the crusts and cut the bread the same way. Pound 2 of the sage leaves with a little salt and incorporate it into the butter. Spread the bread with it. Thread the cut and buttered bread on to the skewers with cubes of veal in between each; also put bits of the remaining fresh sage leaves on the skewers here and there. Grease an ovenproof earthenware dish and lay the skewered meat in it, preheat the oven to 400 or 425°F/200 or 220°C/Gas Mark 6 or 7 and cook for about 20 minutes or less. Serve still on the skewers and spoon over any juices which may have formed in the dish.

Note: Remember that the skewers are very hot, as they have just come out of the oven, so warn your guests, and be sure to provide a napkin to hold them with when removing the meat.

Most Glorious Night

Mandorlata di Peperoni

This dish should be served separately — not on the same plate as the meat. If seedless white grapes are in season use them instead of sultanas.

1 tablespoon sultanas
1 tablespoon white wine (optional)
1 red pepper
2 over-ripe tomatoes
2 tablespoons oil
1 tablespoon flaked almonds
½ tablespoon vinegar
seasoning

Soak the sultanas in the wine (or water) for half an hour. Remove the seeds from the pepper and slice it into thin strips. Peel the tomatoes, scoop out the seeds, cut into small chunks. Heat the oil in a flameproof earthenware or porcelain dish with a lid. Sauté the strips of pepper until softened, add all the other ingredients, cover and simmer for 20 minutes. In my view, this dish is best served tepid, but you can choose to serve it hot, cold or tepid according to your taste or mood. It is equally good either way.

Pasta Shells Tossed in Butter

Cook about 6 ounces of pasta shells in a large saucepan with lots of fast-boiling salted water. Test by tasting to see if it's cooked as the instructions on the packet can be misleading. Drain the pasta, return it to the saucepan, add a knob of butter and toss well. Serve in a very hot dish.

Kiwi with Stem Ginger and Lemon

Prepare this when it is most convenient, it will stand waiting a few hours if need be!

2 kiwi fruit
2 oz/50 g crystallized stem ginger
5 fl oz/150 ml cream
1 tablespoon lemon juice
a little clear honey (optional)

Peel the kiwi fruit, cut them into thin slices, then quarter the slices and halve the quarters. Chop up the ginger into the smallest bits you can manage. Lightly whip the cream until it holds its form, stir in the lemon juice, then fold in the kiwi and ginger. Serve piled into tall wine glasses. I do not add any sugar because I like the contrasting sharpness of the Kiwi and lemon and the hot sweet of the ginger. But if you prefer it a little sweeter I suggest a few drops of clear honey dribbled over the top of each serving as the most delicious way of sweetening it.

Alternatively, simply arrange the halved slices of Kiwi fruit with the chopped ginger in glasses and hand the cream separately.

A Way to a Man's Heart

Duck Liver Sautéd in Cointreau

Roast Loin of Pork Chops
Broad Beans Glazed in Lemon Butter
New Potatoes Steamed on a
Bed of Thyme

Walnut Stuffed Pancakes

Duck liver is a great delicacy in my opinion. It should be saved each time you cook a duck and frozen until you have enough livers to serve as a main course – what luxury! For this menu the liver of one duck is just enough, but two would be much better. If the liver is very small add a couple of whole small firm mushrooms to pad out the dish.

Duck Liver Sautéd in Cointreau

(a mere mouthful with toast)

1 or 2 duck's livers
a little flour
1 scant tablespoon clarified butter
1 or 2 teaspoons Cointreau
salt and pepper

Cut the liver into about 4 pieces, more or less depending on the size of the liver. You want fair-sized bites rather than small bits. Dust very lightly with flour and fry very briefly indeed in the very hot clarified butter (little more than passing them through it really). Just before removing the livers, add the Cointreau to the butter and juices. Season to taste and serve at once with hot buttered toast.

Roast Loin of Pork Chops

It is important to get your butcher to prepare the loin for you. You want the meat in one piece but with the bone cut through so you can carve straight through after cooking, making four thin chops. Also ask him to diamond-score the skin (criss-cross).

4 thin loin of pork chops
plenty of salt
olive oil
1 large cooking apple or 2 medium
*   ones*

About 30 minutes or so before putting the meat in the oven rub the skin vigorously with plenty of salt and leave to stand. Set the oven at 350°F/180°C/Gas Mark 4. This will allow slow roasting, enabling you to leave it in the oven until you are ready to serve it. Wipe the skin quite dry, the salt will have drawn out any moisture there might have been. Rub well with olive oil, then again with salt. Slice the apple, without peeling or coring it, into as many slices as you can; lay them in the roasting tin and stand the pork on them. Put approximately 5 fluid ounces/150 millilitres of water in the dish and place in the middle of the preheated oven. Cook for 40 minutes to the pound plus 20 minutes extra (this timing does not suit all joints of pork, only small ones like this). Strain the apple and juices in the pan, adjust seasoning and serve with the meat.

Broad Beans Glazed in Lemon Butter

If you are buying them in their pods you will need to buy 1¾–2 lb/750–1 kg of beans to be on the safe side.

broad beans
1½ oz/40 g butter
1 dessertspoon lemon juice
1 scant teaspoon clear honey
2 needles of fresh rosemary, finely
*   scissored*
salt and pepper

Pod the beans and plunge them into a small amount of boiling salted water. Cook for barely 5 minutes then drain and refresh under cold water. It is important at this stage to slip off the skins of each bean except those that are very young and tender. Melt the butter, add the beans, lemon juice, rosemary and honey, simmer for a few minutes. Adjust seasoning with a little salt and pepper. Serve hot or tepid.

New Potatoes Steamed on a Bed of Thyme

Wash the potatoes, do not peel them. Line a steamer with a generous bunch of fresh thyme, lay the potatoes on top, sprinkle with salt and cover with more thyme. Steam in the usual way. To serve, lift the thyme off the potatoes, put them in a serving dish and sprinkle with lemon juice.

Walnut Stuffed Pancakes

4 thin pale pancakes
4 oz/100 g ground walnuts
4 oz/100 g cream cheese
1 tablespoon caster sugar
1 small egg, well beaten
2 tablespoons single cream

Combine all the filling ingredients, spread evenly over the pancakes and roll them up. Place in 2 individual ovenproof dishes and spoon 1 tablespoon of cream over each pair. Lay a sheet of greaseproof paper on top and bake in a moderate oven 350°F/180°C/Gas Mark 4 for about 15 to 20 minutes. Serve hot.

This dessert can be prepared in advance and put in the oven when you start the main course if you think you are unlikely to linger. Or, if you prefer a long pause, you can cook it after you have finished the main course. The cooking time is quite flexible, for longer cooking, lower the temperature. As long as the pancakes are heated through and the filling set, it does not matter how long or short the cooking time is.

Easy Does It

Selection of Smoked Meats

Pheasant in the Pot
cooked with Red Kidney Beans
served with Hungarian Cucumber Salad

Crème Brulée Boûle au Liqueur

The minimum of work is required for this menu and it is therefore a most suitable meal to produce in what may be very romantic circumstances but far from ideal culinary ones. Maybe you are on holiday and have no oven, but with just a gas ring, camping stove or even a campfire you can serve this delicious meal. The bird is interchangeable with a small chicken, and rice could be used instead of the beans if you do not have the time to soak or precook the beans – and I really do not recommend the use of canned ones in this dish, as they tend to disintegrate too easily.

Selection of Smoked Meats

This is just a question of choice and then decorative arrangement on a plate. I like to go to a delicatessen and ask for 1 oz/25 g of all the unfamiliar cured or cooked meats and sausages. The only difficulty is in remembering the names of any of them, let alone the ones I find so good that I want to buy them again!

Pheasant in the Pot cooked with Red Kidney Beans

2 heaped tablespoons dried red
*   kidney beans*
1 oz/25 g butter
1 small pheasant well hung (its age
*   is not of great importance as any*
*   bird will come out of this pot*
*   tender)*
2 carrots
3 or 4 large cloves of garlic
1 good-size sprig of fresh sage
1 small sprig of rosemary
salt and pepper
1 scant dessertspoon wine vinegar
1 scant teaspoon tomato purée
½ small cauliflower

Place the kidney beans in the largest pan you can find full of cold water. Boil uncovered for 10 minutes, then reduce heat to simmering point and cook covered, no salt added until the beans are tender. This could be anything from 1 to 2 hours depending on the freshness of the beans. When they are tender, but not mushy or too soft, drain, refresh under cold water and set aside for later use.

Melt the butter in a frying pan and brown as much of the bird as possible in it over a fairly fierce flame, turning it all the time. Remove it to a casserole. Slice the carrots and garlic, and roughly chop the herbs. Add to the casserole and put the giblets, liver and heart inside the bird. Pour in enough water to come one third of the way up the side of the dish, roughly covering the thighs of the bird. Season with salt, pepper and vinegar, cover, bring to simmering point over a flame with a heat defuser on top of it, and cook like this for about 1 hour. Then add the beans (or rice if preferred), tomato purée and cauliflower broken into florets, cover and cook very slowly for a further 20 to 30 minutes, stir from time to time and adjust seasoning. To serve, lift the bird out of the pot and carve thick slices off the breast and a leg each, surround with the juice and vegetables. A hunk of French bread and the following salad is all that's needed.

I hardly need to add that the carcase and any leftover vegetables with wine and water added will make a divine soup for tomorrow.

Hungarian Cucumber Salad

1 small cucumber
1 tablespoon salt
1 teaspoon caster sugar
2 pinches of dill weed
1 teaspoon vinegar
3 or 4 tablespoons single, double or
*   soured cream*
a sprinkle of paprika powder for
*   decoration*

Peel and slice the cucumber as thinly as possible, sprinkle all the salt over it and leave to stand, ideally for at least 1 hour, but it could be less. Pour boiling water over it, drain it at once and squeeze out as much of the liquid as possible with your hands. Place it in a serving dish, sprinkle the sugar, dill and vinegar over while it is still warm and mix well. Cover with the cream (do not mix) and decorate with the pinch of paprika.

Crème Brulée Boûle au Liqueur

This is a way of making a crème brulée without a grill or brulée iron.

3 egg yolks
1 oz/25 g caster sugar
¼ pint/150 ml double cream
2 teaspoons of liqueur of your choice
2 extra heaped dessertspoons caster
*   sugar for the brulée topping*

Beat the sugar and egg yolks together lightly. Scald the cream and pour it slowly over the eggs, stirring all the time; transfer to a bain-marie and thicken over not quite boiling water, stirring continuously. Tip it into 2 individual ramekins or similar pots in which you have put the liqueur of your choice, and chill very thoroughly. Do not cover; this will allow for the formation of a skin; the thicker it is the better. In a thick-bottomed small pan melt the sugar, and as soon as it turns golden pour it over the crèmes quickly; it will set almost at once, thus giving you the desired brulée topping.

A Fine Romance

Parsnip and Orange Soup

Wild Duck with Thyme and Honey
Creamed Jerusalem Artichokes
Sauté Potatoes
Chicory and Walnut Salad

Marinated Italian Figs served with
a Dollop of Cream Creese

I'll never forget the first time I ate teal (wild duck); it was indeed a candlelit dinner for two but I had not done the cooking, he had. Or was there someone else out there? I never found out! Placed before me was this really succulent and delicious looking little duck, glistening and smelling almost as good as it looked. With knife, fork and my customary enthusiasm I lunged at the bird and to my embarrassment it resisted the knife and fork and shot across the table, almost as if still alive! Back on my

plate, many apologies later, I achieved an incision with the knife, but only after a number of tries. To my horror this cut revealed blood-red, or should I say blue, almost cold raw insides. Well I didn't even know then that teal was meant to be underdone, but even if I had known, this was surely overdoing the underdoing? Anyway it was inedible, largely due to the fact that it was impossible to separate the flesh from the bone in even an unladylike manner. Some romance that turned out to be!

Since that day I have not been very enthusiastic about cooking teal the way most books recommend. I prefer to cook it so there is just a hint of pink in the thigh perhaps, no more.

Parsnip and Orange Soup

My only comment on this is that it is very good and can be served either hot or chilled.

½ a smallish onion
8 oz/225 g parsnips
¾ oz/20 g butter
the grated rind of ¼ orange
juice of one small orange
¾ pint/450 ml clear chicken or veal
*   stock*
salt and pepper

Slice the onion finely, cut the parsnips into small pieces (the chipper disc on a food processor is ideal). Sweat the onion and parsnips in the butter, then add the orange rind and juice. Simmer for a second or two and add the stock. Season with salt and pepper, cook gently until the parsnips are soft. Liquidize, then push through a sieve. Reheat or chill and serve. Hot brown rolls go well.

Note: Please do not be tempted to omit putting the soup through a sieve; parsnips often have quite stringy bits that escape the liquidizer blade.

Wild duck with Thyme and Honey

2 small wild ducks
3 or 4 sprigs of thyme
salt and pepper
butter
2 teaspoons clear honey

Push a little of the thyme inside each bird after having washed and dried them inside and out. Crush the remaining thyme with the salt and rub it all over the skin of the birds. Melt the butter and honey together and pour half of it over the birds. Preheat the oven to

350°F/ 180°C/Gas Mark 4 and cook the birds for 35 minutes. Pour the remaining butter and honey over, turn up the heat to maximum and cook for a further 4 minutes. Serve whole, with any juices from the pan poured over.

Creamed Jerusalem Artichokes

I think this is one of my favourite vegetables. I even love them grated raw in salad.

4 oz/350 g Jerusalem artichokes
1 cooked peeled potato
1 tablespoon cream
a nob of butter
salt and pepper
1 teaspoon finely chopped parsley

Parboil the artichokes, refresh under cold water and peel off the skins. Put back in water to cook until soft, then with the potato push through the finest disc of a mouli into a bowl. Stir in the cream, butter, seasoning and parsley, transfer to an ovenproof dish, cover and heat through when required.

Sauté Potatoes

These may be prepared in advance and reheated just before serving. See the method on page 24.

Chicory and Walnut Salad

To counteract the tendency to bitterness in this salad, it is dressed with orange juice and walnut oil only, seasoned of course with sugar, salt and pepper.

Combine one chicory coarsely cut up with a handful of walnut halves and sprinkle with seasoning, orange juice and walnut oil.

If you are unable to find walnut oil you could try the following idea. Crush a few walnuts quite finely and fry them in corn oil or sunflower until quite dark golden, but not burnt, allow to cool and use in place of walnut oil.

Marinated Italian Figs with Cream Cheese

These are canned and very good; one can should be ample.

1 can Italian figs
1 dessertspoon brandy
2 shakes Angostura bitters
1 dessertspoon lemon juice
2 oz/50 g double cream cheese

Mix the brandy, the bitters and the lemon juice with some of the fig juice and pour over the figs. Leave to stand for at least 1 hour at room temperature (but it could be half a day). Put a dollop of soft fresh double cream cheese on top of each portion as you serve it.

Aurum is an Italian orange liqueur and quite hard to find, but, should you have the luck to come across some, use it instead of the brandy lemon and bitters – it is sensational!

Most Glorious Night

Crab Pancakes

Soused Woodpigeon
Summer Spinach
Hot French Bread

Fresh Peaches in White Wine

This menu is ideal for a dinner late on a warm summer's evening, after a visit to an open-air concert perhaps. It is light and can all be prepared even a day ahead without spoiling – in fact, the woodpigeon should be prepared at least two days in advance.

The pancakes are best served hot, but the rest of the food is cold, except for the bread. Do not be tempted to add other dishes or salads, it is not necessary. The first course is rich and filling, and what follows is delicate and simple, which is its virtue. Have confidence in its style; I think you will find it very rewarding.

Crab Pancakes

4 large plain pancakes
6 oz/175 g mixed crabmeat, fresh if
*   possible*
3 oz/75 g fresh cream cheese
½ teaspoon anchovy essence
¼ red pepper
1 teaspoon oil
1 teaspoon mild wine vinegar
1 egg beaten
salt and pepper
1 or 2 tablespoons single cream
fennel feathers

Combine the crabmeat (first having checked carefully that there are no bits of shell left in it) with the cream cheese, and add the anchovy essence. Soften the piece of red pepper in the oil over a gentle heat, then push it through a fine sieve into the crab mixture. Add the vinegar and beaten egg, season and mix well. (If it should be too runny to handle add a few fresh white breadcrumbs, but this is not normally necessary.) Divide the mixture into 4 and roll it up in the pancakes, which should be placed seam down in a shallow gratin dish – or 2 individual ones would be even better because it makes it much easier to serve and quicker to cook. To cook, spoon the cream over, heat the oven to 375 or 400°F/190 or 200°C/Gas Mark 5 or 6 and bake for about 15 or 20 minutes; lay a piece of greaseproof paper lightly over the top to avoid the pancakes going crisp. Scissor the fennel over as you serve.

Soused Woodpigeon

Woodpigeon is best towards the end of summer, but this method of cooking would turn the toughest of old birds into succulent tender delicacies!

2 tablespoons olive oil
2 woodpigeons
1 small onion finely grated
2 cloves of garlic finely grated
1 heaped tablespoon salt
10 peppercorns
a fair-sized sprig of rosemary
4 cardamom seeds broken open
½ teaspoon ground allspice
1 tablespoon muscovado sugar
¼ pint/150 ml light dry red wine
¼ pint/150 ml wine vinegar
½ pint/300 ml water

Heat the oil in a frying pan and brown the pigeons over a fierce heat, then place them in an earthenware casserole. In the same frying pan and oil, gently fry the onion and garlic until transparent and tip them on top of the pigeons. Add the salt, peppercorns, rosemary (cut up with scissors) cardamom, allspice and sugar. Combine all the liquids together in a saucepan and bring to the boil, then tip at once over the pigeons. Place the casserole over a gentle heat and bring to simmering point, cover and cook thus for 35 minutes, turning the birds over at least twice or more during cooking. Remove from the heat, turn the birds breast side down in the liquids and leave to cool very slowly, wrapping a couple of towels over the casserole to ensure really slow cooling. When cold, refrigerate the whole casserole for at least 2 days – better still 5 days – before serving. Turn the birds twice a day if possible. To serve, slice all the meat off the bone as thinly as possible and put a little of the onion on each portion; discard the liquid.

Summer Spinach

This dish has to have fresh basil. It is not always the easiest herb to find in the shops but it is surprisingly easy to grow during the spring and summer months. The secret is not to put it in the open ground unless you are really certain of a hot, hot summer. Grow it on a sunny indoor windowsill. Pick it from the top (the growing tips in fact) very frequently and feed and water it almost daily. Have several pots, the larger the better, because the bigger the pot the bigger the plants. Two or three plants to a pot maximum.

The second thing this dish has to have is very fresh spinach – frozen simply will not do.

1½ lb/675 g fresh spinach
a good handful of fresh basil
salt and pepper
2 teaspoons lemon juice
a generous sprinkling of allspice
1 egg
5 fl oz/150 ml good full-cream
  fresh yogurt
1 teaspoon grated parmesan cheese
a pinch of paprika

Wash and trim the spinach. Blanch it in plenty of boiling water for a couple of minutes or so, drain it, refresh under cold water then squeeze out all the liquid you possibly can. If you have a food processor chop the spinach in it, but do not purée it. Add the fresh basil while processing. If you do not have a processor, chop the spinach as finely as you can with a chopping knife on a wooden board, adding the basil as you do so. Put the chopped spinach and basil in an oiled ovenproof dish that is not too deep and is attractive enough to bring to table. Season with salt, pepper, lemon and allspice. Pat the spinach down to level and compress it slightly and smooth the top. Beat the egg into the yogurt and carefully pour it on top of the spinach. Sprinkle the parmesan over and decorate with the pinch of paprika. Bake in a preheated oven 350°F/180°C/Gas Mark 4 until the yogurt has set but not coloured, about 20 minutes or a little longer. Serve tepid or cold, both of which are infinitely superior to hot. Do not worry if you see liquid round the spinach when you take it from the oven; this will be re-absorbed as the dish cools.

Fresh Peaches in White Wine

I favour the dark orange Italian peaches for flavour. I also favour a Sicilian wine, but this is a matter for personal taste. A tart peach with a sweet wine is rather good, on the other hand a sweet peach with a really dry wine is most interesting. Do not be tempted to use some inferior plonk; it will be horrible and most 'unspecial'! Peel the peaches and cut in half round the crease. Remove the stones by twisting the halves in opposite directions. Slice them very thinly and arrange them in an ever-decreasing circle in individual shallow bowls. Pour the wine over to just cover the peach and leave for several hours. Just before serving float a small flower in the centre, such as summer jasmine.

Getting to Know You

Pâté de la Maison

Grilled Steaks of Fresh Salmon
Courgettes (or marrow) in Dill Sauce
Small Potatoes Roasted in their Skins

Black Cherries and Sour Cream

This is a fairly conventional menu, which is not a bad idea if you are not too sure of the tastes of the person you are cooking for. It is the style with which you present the meal that will reveal most about you! There is also a good chance that the courgettes in dill sauce will be something new, unless your guest is familiar with Hungarian cuisine, which has a similar dish using marrow.

The pâté may be cooked in advance and the courgettes also. The salmon can be prepared for cooking ahead of time and the black cherry dessert should be chilled for a while beforehand, so there is very little to do at the last minute.

Pâté de la Maison

3 juniper berries
2 teaspoons gin
4 oz/100 g chicken liver
2 oz/50 g fatty bacon
2 fat cloves of garlic (4 if they are
*   small and rather dry)*
1 scant teaspoon green peppercorns
2 oz/50 g butter
1 teaspoon lemon juice
clarified butter

Soak the juniper berries in the gin for 30 minutes. Clean the livers, making certain there are no bitter green bits. Coarsely chop the livers, the bacon and the garlic. In a barely greased frying pan fry the bacon with the garlic until well coloured, then add the livers, stir them about for a few minutes to cook them all over, but only lightly, stir in the juniper berries and green peppercorns just before pulling off the heat. Leave to cool. If you have a blender or food processor the next step will be quick and easy. Put all the ingredients in it, including the butter which should now be soft but not melted, and process to a smooth cream, taste and adjust seasoning. If you do not have either a processor or blender you will have to use the finest disc of a mouli or push it all through a fine sieve, then beat in the butter and lemon, adjust seasoning and tip into a little pot with a lid if possible. Press a sprig of rosemary into the top for decoration and pour clarified butter over. Chill.

Serve with hot thin brown toast. I would not offer butter, it does not need it.

Grilled Steaks of Fresh Salmon

This dish can be partly prepared in advance.

2 salmon steaks
4 small white mushrooms
1 teaspoon finely chopped fennel
*   feathers*
2 teaspoons lemon juice
salt and pepper
1 oz/25 g butter

Cut 2 pieces of foil twice the size of the steaks and grease them with butter. Lay the salmon on one half. Slice the mushrooms very thinly and lay them on top of the salmon, sprinkle the fennel and lemon juice over, season with salt and plenty of pepper and fold over the foil, completely sealing in the salmon (you will need the butter later). You could now put the parcels in the fridge until just before cooking them. Heat the grill fully, place the parcels upside down – that is with the mushrooms underneath – cook thus for 3 minutes, turn them over, cook a further 3 minutes, then open the foil and finish off cooking. Pop the butter in as you open the foil; by the time it has completely melted the salmon steaks will be cooked and should be served at once.

Courgettes in Dill Sauce

This dish is ideal for overgrown courgettes and, of course, marrow, although I do not find the flavour of marrow as good as the courgettes. You can reheat this dish, so you can make it ahead of time.

12 oz/350 g courgettes
1 oz/25 g butter
1 oz/25 g plain flour
approx. 2 pint/150 ml chicken stock
1 teaspoon lemon juice
½ teaspoon sugar
½ teaspoon mild French mustard
½ teaspoon dill weed
1 tablespoon single or double cream
plenty of salt

Unless the courgettes are very young, peel them, slit them in half lengthways and, using a teaspoon, scoop out the seeds and soft pulp surrounding them. Grate or shred the peeled courgettes with a coarse grater or a food processor and sprinkle them generously with plenty of salt; leave to stand a while to draw out the liquid. Melt the butter in a saucepan, add the flour, stir and cook a little, then slowly add the stock, lemon, sugar and mustard. Stir well; the sauce should be fairly thick because the courgettes will dilute it. Rinse the courgettes and squeeze out as much liquid as possible, pat dry with a kitchen towel and then tip into the sauce, adding the dill weed at the same time. Stir continuously until it bubbles, cook for 3 or 4 minutes then add the cream and adjust seasoning. Serve warm or hot.

Small Potatoes Roasted in their Skins

Look for smooth, evenly shaped small potatoes. Wash and dry them, place in an ovenproof earthenware dish, pour olive oil over, sprinkle with salt and plenty of slightly crushed coriander seed, place in a hot oven 425 or 450°F/220 or 230°C/Gas Mark 7 or 8. Cook for about 45 minutes to 1 hour depending on the size of the potatoes.

Black Cherries and Sour Cream

This is not quite what it sounds, except it is incredibly easy, involves no cooking and, I am ashamed to say, in my view comes under the heading of cheating!

4 large ginger-nut biscuits
3 tablespoons cherry brandy
1 jar or can of black cherries –
  approx. 1 lb/450 g
2 heaped tablespoons sour cream

Place the biscuits whole in 2 individual serving bowls and spoon the liqueur over them. Strain the cherries, retaining the juice. Spoon over the biscuits as much juice as they can absorb. Be careful not to squash them. Arrange the cherries on top so as to conceal them completely and put a dollop of sour cream on the very top. Chill until needed. Remove from the fridge 30 minutes before serving.

Simple is Beautiful

Simple is Beautiful

Fish Terrine

A Really Mixed Salad
Veal Chops and Penne

Mikki's Syllabub

Fish terrine is a fairly light first course that goes well before these veal chops. As you probably know, veal chops tend to be rather large and filling. Penne is a type of pasta. The word is Italian for quills, meaning the part one used to write with, not the feather as many an English translation of *penne* on menus in Italy will have it! If you cannot find penne, macaroni would do.

The terrine and the syllabub can be made in advance, but not the main course, although it does not take very long to prepare and is quite straightforward. Vividly coloured plates, if you have some, perhaps rarely used, would complement the pasta and veal, which have little colour of their own.

Fish Terrine

8 oz/225 g fresh haddock
2 cloves of garlic
1 tablespoon chopped parsley
6 tablespoons double cream
2 teaspoons lemon juice
1 egg
6 oz/175 g fresh salmon
6 oz/175 g peeled prawns
1 can of anchovies
salt and pepper

Remove the skin and all the bones from the haddock, break it into pieces and put it in a food processor with the garlic, parsley, cream, lemon juice and egg; process just long enough to chop and combine all the ingredients without turning them to a purée. This can be done by hand in the absence of a food processor. Simply chop everything very finely and combine them altogether in a bowl with the liquids, beating well. Remove the skin and bone from the salmon and break it into small pieces. Butter a small terrine – or a soufflé dish would do. Divide the haddock mixture in half, put half of it in the terrine, pressing it well down and

levelling it. Place a layer of salmon on top of it, then all the prawns evenly arranged. On top of the prawns put half of the anchovy fillets, then cover with the rest of the salmon. Press well down and put in the remaining haddock mixture, smooth the top over and arrange the remaining anchovies in a criss-cross pattern on the top. Cover with buttered greaseproof paper and foil or a lid, place in the oven in a bain-marie at 300°F/150°C/ Gas Mark 2 and cook for 1 hour and 10 minutes. Allow to cool, then chill thoroughly, for not less than 2 hours, before serving. To serve, cut a thick slice and offer it with hot brown toast. A spray or two of fennel feathers make a decorative garnish.

Note: It is a personal choice as to whether you turn out the terrine. Usually I prefer not to, as it keeps fresher remaining in the dish it has cooked in.

A Really Mixed Salad

You could prepare most of the salad a little ahead of time and put it in the fridge, leaving only the avocado and dressing to do at the last minute.

approx. 2 mushrooms
part of a firm, crisp lettuce, such as
*   iceberg*
1 bunch of watercress
fresh basil
1 clove of garlic
a few radishes
a few seedless white grapes
a little grated carrot
2 oz/50 g walnut halves
juice of 1 lime
a sprinkle of sugar and salt
1 small ripe avocado
walnut oil

Slice the mushrooms and scissor the lettuce, watercress and basil. Finely chop (do not crush) the garlic, thinly slice the radishes, peel and cut the avocado in chunks. Combine all the ingredients trickling the walnut oil over last of all.

Veal Chops and Penne

When I first created this recipe I served it to an Italian gentleman who paid me the compliment of asking me for the recipe so he could give it to his mother to cook! Just what I wanted to hear!

2 oz/50 g butter
2 veal chops
flour for coating
a sprig of fresh rosemary or a pinch
*   of dried*
5 tablespoons light red Rioja wine
*   (it must be light red)*
salt and pepper
1 tablespoon lemon juice
1 clove of garlic, thinly sliced
5 tablespoons cream
approx. 6 oz/175 g penne

Melt the butter in a large frying pan. Coat the chops in seasoned flour, fry them on both sides to seal them, then add the rosemary, wine, salt, pepper, lemon juice and garlic. Stir, bring to simmering point and add the cream, cover and simmer while you cook the penne in plenty of fast-boiling salted water. Taste to tell when they are cooked to your liking – not soft and soggy, I hope! Drain well and dribble just a few drops of oil over, mix at once to prevent the penne sticking together. Tip into a warmed serving dish, pile the chops on top and pour the sauce all over.

Mikki's Syllabub

½ pint/150 ml double cream
3 tablespoons sherry
1 tablespoon brandy
1 tablespoon lemon juice
1 oz/25 g caster sugar

Lightly whip the cream; as it begins to thicken add all the other ingredients, watching very carefully that you do not overwhip the cream, which will ruin the taste and texture. The consistency should be light and fluffy, just holding its form. Pile the syllabub into tall slender wine glasses and chill. Serve with a langue de chat.

The Way to a Woman's Heart

Fort Worth Very Finest Steak Burgers
served with
Hungarian Style Potatoes and a
Tomato Salad with Garlic Croûtons

Fresh Figs gently cooked in
Wine and Honey, served with
Lemon Soured Cream

Now I have come to one menu that is meant especially for an inexperienced but willing man to cook. By that I do not mean to imply that this book is meant only for women, it is just that I think that women are far more imaginative and therefore more romantic than most men and will be

more inclined to be interested in it. Having said that, nothing would give me greater pleasure than to be proved wrong, by actions, of course!

There is no starter; I don't think he has the time unless it is something simple like grapefruit juice!

Fort Worth Very Finest Steak Burgers

One summer a delicious, slightly dotty American musician arrived in the neighbourhood. Would I take him to a good butcher, because he wanted to cook a meal for me? I couldn't believe my ears, no one ever seems to want to cook for me and in my kitchen, what's more. Jolly romantic too, I can tell you, with my two young children joining in the fun! To come to the point, David came from Fort Worth, Texas, and cooked these burgers, which were terrific, and I must say it was a pleasure to watch him making them. Hence their name.

1 sprig of rosemary
4 fresh basil leaves (or ¼ teaspoon dried)
2 sage leaves
1 sprig of marjoram
1 sprig thyme
2 small sprigs parsley
¼ teaspoon salt and plenty of black pepper
1 lb /450 g best rump steak minced (anything from Texas is big!)

Place all the herbs with the salt and pepper in a coffee grinder and grind until very fine. Knead the meat really well on a flat surface. Divide in two, knead again, then tunnel a hole with your thumb to the centre of the ball of meat, fill it with a good pinch of the herbs, then squeeze and pat it together again to make a really compact, firm ball of meat. Heat a little fat in a frying pan and, over a fierce heat, sear the burgers on all sides to seal them, transfer them to an ovenproof dish with a lid and finish off the cooking in a very hot oven 450°F/230°C/Gas Mark 8 for about 5–15 minutes. The length of time depends on how you like your steak cooked – rare, medium or well done.

Hungarian Style Potatoes

1 lb /450 g cooked peeled potatoes
1 tablespoon white wine vinegar
1 oz /25 g lard
½ teaspoon paprika
1 pinch of caraway seeds
1 bayleaf
½ teaspoon salt
4 tablespoons sour cream

Take a quarter of the cooked potato and mash it with the vinegar. Heat the lard, draw the pan off the heat, stir in the paprika, then add the mashed potato. If it is too thick add a little stock or milk. Stir, add the caraway seeds, bay leaf and salt. Cut the remaining potatoes into chunks and heat them through in the potato sauce. Stir in the sour cream just before serving.

Tomato Salad with Garlic Croûtons

(almost every man's favourite)

2 or 3 large tomatoes
salt and pepper
1 teaspoon wine vinegar
2 or 3 tablespoons olive oil
2 fairly thick slices of bread
2 cloves of garlic

Peel the tomatoes if you think the skin is at all tough (plunge them in and out of boiling water and the skins almost fall off), cut them into chunks and put in a bowl, sprinkle with salt, pepper and vinegar and set aside. Heat the oil, cube the bread, having removed the crusts, slice the garlic and fry it in the oil. When it turns golden, add the bread and fry it, stirring it until it is really crisp and golden all over. Keep it in the frying pan until just before serving, then reheat it and pour 'sizzling' over the tomatoes. Do not mix.

Note: The quality of the olive oil is always important and especially so here. My choice, whenever possible, is the dark green virgin olive oil from Greece or Cyprus. It is the least expensive and, for me, the best. Should it be too strong or too heavy for some recipes or tastes, I dilute it with sunflower oil, thus making it a very flexible and useful commodity.

Fresh Figs in Wine and Honey with Lemon Soured Cream

I have a passion for fresh figs. My first honeymoon was spent in the South of France, on a carnation farm in the hills behind Nice. Our tent was pitched underneath a fig tree heavily laden with the ripe fruit. It was then that I learned the joys of cooked figs, for they fell from their branches day and night. To ring the changes I cooked them in various different ways, this being one of them.

6 or 8 fresh figs (depending on their
*   size, even more if small)*
enough dry Italian rosé wine to cover
1 or 2 tablespoons honey
1 teaspoon lemon juice
4 tablespoons thick double cream

Place the figs in a small saucepan and just cover them with wine, add the honey and bring to boiling point, then simmer until the figs are really tender. Cool and chill. Stir the lemon into the thick cream and serve it with the figs.

Just a Soupçon?

A Fantastic Seafood Soup with
Garlic Bread
Followed by a Variation on
Tarte Tatin

This may sound a simple menu. It is, and all the better for being so. This seafood soup could not possibly be followed by anything other than a dessert and/or cheese. To do it justice you must have generous helpings and that in turn leaves little desire or space for anything else! It cannot be prepared in a rush, it must not be. You will need time to take the trouble required, but I can promise you it will be one of the most unusual and successful dinners of all time. Whoever you serve it to will want the recipe — don't tell them, just give them this book.

Fantastic Seafood Soup

1 red chilli
2 small red peppers
1 onion
5 tablespoons olive oil
about 1½ lb/675 g mixed seafood,
    such as:
    1 red mullet; 1 small whiting;
    2 oz/50 g whitebait; 2 oz/50 g
    mussels and cockles (out of their
    shells); 4 large prawns in their
    shells; a small piece of monk fish;
    4 scallops; 1 fresh sardine;
    1 oz/25 g shrimps (The list could
    go on and on, and it is not
    necessary to follow it exactly. Just
    use it as a guide and don't worry
    too much about exact weight at
    this stage.)
1 14 oz (396 g) can of tomatoes
4 tablespoons red wine vinegar
1 teaspoon anchovy essence
seasoning

Cut open the chilli and, leaving it whole, remove the seeds. Quarter the peppers and remove the seeds. Chop the onion fairly coarsely. Heat the oil and gently sauté the onion, peppers and chilli. Now prepare the seafood. If you have bought mussels in their shells clean them as follows: scrub them well and put them in a bowl under running cold water for at least 15 minutes. Remove any beards. Dry them and place in a hot oven for a few minutes until the shells have opened (discard any which do not). When cool remove the mussels from their shells.

Cut all the fish (not the whitebait and prawns) into bite-size pieces, being very diligent about removing bones and scales. It is quite in order to leave the skin on the smaller fish such as the mullet and sardine providing you have been meticulous about scaling. When the peppers and chilli have softened remove them from the pan and push them through a fine sieve, returning the resultant pulp back to the pan with the onion still in it. (You may choose to discard the chilli at this stage rather than putting it through the sieve, it all depends on how 'hot' you like your food. I always leave it in.) Push the tomatoes through a sieve or mouli to remove the seeds and any skins; add them to the peppers and onion. Bring to simmering point, add the vinegar and anchovy essence, bring to boiling point and add all the fish except the mussels, cockles and prawns. Boil for about 15 minutes, add the mussels, cockles and prawns, adjust seasoning if necessary and cook for a further 5 minutes. Transfer to a hot tureen and bring to table with a ladle plunged ready for helping oneself.

Garlic bread

If you cannot get a French stick of bread, another very tasty way of making a different kind of garlic bread is as follows. Cut fairly thick slices of crusty white bread, combine together very thoroughly butter, crushed garlic (lots!) and plenty of finely chopped parsley and spread a thick layer on each piece of bread. Bake it in a hot oven until crisp, and serve hot.

Tarte Tatin Variation

This is the apple tart which is turned upside down. When you come to think about it it is such an obvious thing to do. How many times have you made or tasted apple tarts, pies or flans where the pastry at the bottom is pale and soggy or even hard and really quite disagreeable? This way it is perfect every time and well worth the extra trouble.

For the pastry
6 oz/175 g plain flour
4 oz/100 g butter
1 teaspoon caster sugar
1 very small egg yolk
approx. 1 tablespoon cold water

For the filling
8 large cooking apples
3 firm pears
½ teaspoon cinnamon
1 tablespoon soft brown sugar

Sift the flour, cut the butter into small pieces and with your finger tips work it into the flour until it resembles breadcrumbs. Mix in the sugar. Combine the egg and water, tip it into the flour mixture and quickly mix and knead to a smooth dough. Chill for 20 minutes.

Peel, core and slice the apples and pears very, very thinly, keeping them covered with salted water to prevent discolouration (it does not harm the flavour). Line the base of a 7-inch/18-centimetre loose-bottomed cake tin with buttered greaseproof paper, grease the sides. Sprinkle some cinnamon and brown sugar on the base. Starting with the pears, lay the slices evenly round and round, slightly overlapping and completely covering the bottom of the tin, and press down. When you have used all the pears continue with the apples; half way through spread a layer of sugar and cinnamon all over and carry on laying the apples to form a flat firm even mound of apple filling inside the cake tin. Roll out the pastry so that it covers the apples but fits inside the rim of the tin. Place the cake tin in a roasting dish (to catch the juice which will run out) and bake in a preheated oven at 375°F/190°C/Gas Mark 5 for 45 minutes. If the pastry begins to colour too much lay a double layer of greaseproof paper over it. To serve, allow to cool just a little, then invert it and turn out. And so the pastry is at the bottom!

Garnish with slices of raw green apple and place a japonica bloom in the centre.

Serve with slightly whipped cream to which you have added a teaspoon of lemon juice.

Time for Talk

Taramasalata
Humus
Marinated Mushrooms
Little Fish Kebabs
Stuffed Spinach or Vine Leaves
Messinia Sausages
Keftethes
Tomato and Feta
Stuffed Squid
Lamb in Wine and Coriander
Black-eyed Beans
Cucumber Salad
Beetroot Salad
Cauliflower Salad
Pitta Bread, Olives, Pickled Chillis

Athenian Cheese Cake

I have heard people, on returning from holiday, bemoaning the lack of variety in Greek food. 'Wonderful country, sea, weather, people, but oh dear, their food, all that oil!' This is not my experience. I find a simplicity in Greek, particularly Cypriot, cooking that is most attractive, and it has style.

The following menu, very much influenced by the Greek meze but by no means authentic, is probably the most versatile in the book. You could select just the dishes which require no last-minute attention at all, they would be mostly cold or tepid and possibly ideal for out-of-doors eating. Or you could select just a few and serve them in the conventional way, with first and second course. Or, best of all, choose a fairly large selection and bring them all to table at once and leave yourself free from the kitchen for the rest of the evening. There is one other way; if you have a willing chum or child, have them discreetly bring the dishes in at various intervals, one or two at a time. A lot of fun can be had that way when quite unexpected dishes appear, no warning having been given, of course! As long as chum disappears for the rest of the evening, this must surely be the most romantic of all candlelit dinners. With just a hint of Mikis Theodorakis music somewhere in the background, what more could one do to set the scene? Nothing; you will have created a stunning occasion.

I am going to list and give recipes (where needed) for more dishes than it is necessary to prepare for one evening. Make your own selection, mixing hot and cold dishes if possible and giving a fairly wide choice, say about nine separate items, that includes things you do not have to cook but simply put on a dish – for example, big black juicy olives.

Taramasalata

(anglicized version and the best!)

4 oz/100 g smoked cod's roe
1 or 2 large cloves of garlic
2 or 3 tablespoons fresh lemon juice
plenty of olive oil
boiling water
parsley for garnish

I would not personally care to make this without the aid of either a blender or food processor, though of course it is perfectly possible to do so. Soak the piece of cod's roe in water for about 30 minutes to enable you to peel off the skin. Place it in a blender or food processor with the garlic which you have chopped as finely as possible, add the lemon juice and process until you have a smooth paste. Then begin adding the olive oil fairly slowly. Continue adding the oil until the mixture is so thick it forms great lumps round the bowl. Still processing, add sufficient boiling water to produce a creamy thick mousse-like texture.

Tip into a container with a lid, dribble a little oil over the top and chill until needed. To serve, pile it into a pottery bowl and scissor a little parsley over it. Hot pitta bread is a must with it.

Humus

This can be made very quickly from canned chick peas if you wish, but I prefer using dried ones.

4 oz/100 g chick peas
2 cloves of garlic
1 tablespoon sesame paste (tahini)
  (Obtainable from Greek shops
  and healthfood shops)
1 tablespoon lemon juice
3 tablespoons olive oil
salt and pepper
½ teaspoon cumin seed

Wash the chick peas and bring them to the boil in plenty of unsalted water, simmer for about 2½ hours very gently (this is an alternative to soaking them overnight and then cooking them). When they are tender, strain them, retaining some of the liquid for later use. Place them in a blender or food processor with 1 of the garlic cloves, the sesame paste, the lemon juice, 2 tablespoons of the oil, salt and pepper and process until you have a thick creamy consistency; if it is too dry add some of the cooking liquid. Tip into a container with a lid and chill until needed. It will not keep more than a couple of days.

To serve, finely chop the remaining clove of garlic and, with the cumin seed, fry it in the remaining tablespoon of oil until slightly burnt; put the humus in a pretty serving bowl and tip the burnt cumin and garlic over the top – do not mix it in. Again, hot pitta bread is essential.

Marinated Mushrooms

4 oz/100 g button mushrooms or the
  smallest, freshest closed ones you
  can find
1 tablespoon water with ½ teaspoon
  salt in it
1 tablespoon olive oil
1 tablespoon lemon juice
1 bay leaf

Plunge the mushrooms into just-boiling water for 1 minute only. In a small saucepan, place 1 tablespoon of the boiling water, add the salt and transfer the mushrooms to it. Add the oil, lemon juice and bay leaf, bring to simmering point, then remove from the heat at once, leave to cool and stand for 1 hour.

Lift the mushrooms out of the liquid to serve.

Little Fish Kebabs

This is a very simple dish to make.

4 oz/100 g monk fish
a marinade made from:
  1 tablespoon lemon juice
  two tablespoons olive oil
  some very finely chopped thyme
  and rosemary
  salt and pepper

Cut the monk fish into cubes and drop them in the marinade for a minute or two. Thread them on to the skewers and grill, turning, for barely 5 minutes.

Stuffed Spinach or Vine Leaves

1 tablespoon oil
2 oz/50 g basmati rice
3 tablespoons hot chicken stock
4 oz/100 g cooked chopped chicken
1 clove of garlic chopped
pinch of cinnamon
a generous grating of nutmeg
salt and pepper
2 teaspoons sesame seeds
10 good whole untorn spinach leaves
  or vine leaves
the juice of one whole lemon

Heat the oil and add the rice to it, fry gently, stirring to coat all the grains. Add the stock, and cook over a low heat until it has been absorbed. The rice will not be fully cooked at this point. Allow it to cool in the pan, then combine it with the chicken, adding the garlic, cinnamon, nutmeg, salt and pepper. Dry fry the sesame seeds and add them also to the chicken mixture.

Trim the stalks from the spinach and pour boiling water all over to soften the leaves. Drain them. Put a dollop of the chicken mixture in the centre of the leaves and roll up from the stalk end, folding in the sides as you go to form a smallish tight parcel, place seam down in a small casserole. Pack tightly together in more than one layer if necessary. Trickle a little oil over, then pour over the lemon juice and an equal amount of water. Cover and cook in the oven, preheated to 450°F/230°C/Gas Mark 8 for 15 minutes, then reduce the heat to 250°F/120°C/Gas Mark 1 and cook for a further 45 minutes. Serve tepid or cold.

Messinia Sausages

Your butcher will probably let you have sausage casing. A couple of metres should do; talk it over with him and see what he thinks. To make less than 1 lb (450 g) is not worth while, but I do not think you need to cook them all if you are making other dishes from this menu.

1 lb/450 g lean pork cut from the leg
4 oz/100 g pork back fat
1 tablespoon finely grated orange
  peel

½ teaspoon coarsely ground black
pepper
½ teaspoon chopped thyme
1 teaspoon chopped savory
1 clove of garlic, finely chopped
1 teaspoon salt

Mince the lean pork on the coarse cutter. Cut the fat into small pieces by hand and combine the two. Add the other ingredients to the meat and mix very well. Find a funnel, and then a wooden spoon handle the right size to fit into its neck. Having thoroughly washed the casings, thread them on to the neck of the funnel, ruching them up as far as possible. Leave the bottom end loose and open. Now push the meat into the casing with the aid of the spoon handle, allowing the casing to slip slowly off as you go. Be patient and be prepared to laugh, but know it is worth it in the end! Fold the length of the sausage in 2 or even 3, and pinch together and twist round every 4 or 5 inches (13 or 15 centimetres) to form sausages of the size you like. Hang in an airy place for 2 hours at least before cooking in the usual way – always without pricking.

Keftethes

(meat balls, small, crisp and moist!)

6 oz/175 g minced lean beef or veal
(or even lamb)
1 slice of bread
6 chives
1 teaspoon finely chopped parsley
2 teaspoons chopped fresh mint
1 egg, beaten
salt and pepper
flour for coating
oil for frying

Soak the bread in water and squeeze it out. Scissor the chives. Mix all the ingredients together except the flour and the oil. Knead them firmly and vigorously with your hands. With the aid of teaspoons, if need be, form small firm balls and roll them in the flour. Fry in the hot oil until crisp and brown.

Serve hot, tepid, or even cold.

Tomato and Feta

This is the simple combination of the Cypriot feta cheese crumbled over peeled, ripe chunks of tomato and liberally dressed with Greek olive oil, black olives and lots of fresly ground black pepper.

Stuffed Squid

(tubes of)

1 oz/25 g lean bacon finely minced
1 teaspoon tomato purée
½ slice of bread, crumbed
¼ teaspoon finely chopped rosemary
1 small clove of garlic very finely
chopped
salt and pepper
4 oz/100 g squid tubes (often sold in
supermarkets on their own)
a mixture of oil and butter for frying
flour for dusting with

Combine all the stuffing ingredients and beat them well together. Using a teaspoon to help you, stuff the squid tubes and close the open end with a wooden toothpick. Dust with flour and fry very slowly in the oil and butter (this should take about 20 minutes) then transfer to a warmed serving dish and pour the pan juices over.

Serve hot with wedges of lemon.

Lamb in Wine and Coriander

the knuckle end of half a leg of lamb
1 small onion coarsely chopped
4 whole peeled cloves of garlic
¼ pint/150 ml good red wine
    (Othello from Cyprus is ideal)
salt and pepper
an earthenware casserole or
    saucepan is vital for this dish

In a lightly oiled frying pan sear all sides of the piece of lamb over a fierce heat. Then place it in the casserole, adding all the other ingredients. Cover and put in a very hot oven 475°F/240°C/Gas Mark 9. After 15 minutes turn the heat down to 250°F/120°C/Gas Mark 1 and cook for 2 hours. The meat should just fall off the bone to serve!

Black-eyed Beans

As enjoyed in Paphos, Cyprus. This dish is best eaten tepid, as are so many of the vegetable dishes from Cyprus and Greece.

4 oz/100 g dried black-eyed beans
½ teaspoon salt
a sprig of fresh coriander leaves, or
    fresh marjoram if you cannot find
    coriander
a teaspoon of capers
1 dessertspoon of lemon juice
2 tablespoons good Greek olive oil

Wash the beans thoroughly and place them in a large saucepan of unsalted cold water, bring to the boil, cover and simmer for about 2½ hours, add salt 10 minutes before cooking is completed. Drain the beans and, while still hot, combine them with all the other ingredients and cover. Leave to cool before serving.

Cucumber Salad

Another dish from Paphos

1 small cucumber
1 clove of garlic
12 good fresh mint leaves (or a big
    pinch of dried)
¼ teaspoon sugar
salt to taste
¼ pint/150 ml yogurt

Peel the cucumber and coarsely grate it, sprinkle with salt and set aside to drain off excess liquid. Crush the garlic and mint together with a pestle and mortar, adding the sugar and a little salt only to make the task easier. Squeeze out the cucumber, taste to check it is not too salty (if it is, rinse it briefly and squeeze out again). Combine all the ingredients together in a serving dish. Decorate with an extra mint leaf, finely chopped and sprinkled over.

Beetroot Salad

1 freshly cooked beetroot
1 small egg yolk
2 teaspoons strong Dijon mustard
¼ whole nutmeg, freshly grated
salt to taste
2 tablespoons lemon juice
approx. ¼ pint/150 ml half olive oil
    and half sunflower oil

Cube the beetroot. Beat the egg yolk with the mustard, add the

Just a Soupçon

nutmeg, salt and half the lemon juice. Add the oil a drop at a time as you would for mayonnaise. When it has thickened add the rest of the lemon juice. Pour over the beetroot and serve.

Cauliflower Salad

2 tablespoons lemon juice
2 tablespoons oil
1 teaspoon oregano
salt and pepper
1 very small head of cauliflower or
*   part of one*

Combine the oil, lemon, salt, pepper and oregano. Steam the cauliflower so that it is only just done, with lots of bite to it. Break into florets, put them in a warmed dish with a lid to it. Tip the dressing over the hot cauliflower and put the lid on at once. Serve when cold or tepid.

Athenian Cheese Cake

This cheese cake is made special by the use of Hymettus honey. Try to find it if possible, but if you fail choose a honey with a really distinctive taste of its own.

The base
1 oz/25 g butter
2 oz/50 g ground almonds
8 oz/225 g digestive biscuits,
*   crumbed*

The filling
4 eggs
1 lb/450 g cream cheese
2 oz/50 g plain flour
4 tablespoons Hymettus honey
the grated rind and juice of 1 lemon
8 fl oz/250 ml sour cream or thick
*   yogurt*

Grease the bottom and sides of an 8-inch (20-centimetre) cake tin with the butter. Combine the almonds and crumbed biscuits and spread over the bottom and sides of the cake tin. Separate the eggs. Beat the yolks and, still beating lightly, add the cream cheese, flour,

honey, lemon rind and juice. Beat together thoroughly. Whip the egg whites with a pinch of salt until stiff then fold the cheese mixture into them, using a spatula. Now fold in the sour cream or yogurt. Pour the mixture into the prepared cake tin and bake at 325°F/160°C/ Gas Mark 3 for 45 minutes. Cool and then chill for 8 hours in the cake tin before serving.

Spoil Her

Red and White Fondue
(Steak and Chicken)
with Sauces Blanches et Rouges
Jacket Potatoes or French Bread
Salade Niçoise

Avocado and Lime Chantilly

Should you, while flicking through this book, happen to recall your brother or son asking your advice about cooking a special dinner for his new girlfriend, I suggest that next time you see him you hand him this book open at this page. If he can cook at all he can certainly produce either of these two fondues.

As a fondue can last a whole evening if you want it to, and since it is a dish you would offer only to someone you are certain really enjoys meat, you would be wise to buy slightly more meat then you would if you were going to cook it in the normal way.

The Meat

12oz/350 g fillet* steak
12oz/350 g boned and skinned breast
　of chicken
50-50 oil and butter to half fill the
　fondue pan

*You can use rump steak, but only if you are absolutely certain it will be melt-in-the-mouth tender. Nothing is less romantic than sitting opposite your partner while he furiously masticates, dying to go on talking to you but really wishing you would look the other way just long enough to enable him to remove the offending morsel of meat.

The Sauces

There is no point in offering hot sauces as they would become cold in no time at all; anyway the meat is so hot it needs a cool sauce to enable it to be eaten!

Paprikas Sauce
(pronounced paprikash)

½ a small onion
1 red pepper
½ tablespoon oil
½ teaspoon paprika
½ tablespoon wine vinegar
salt and pepper

Slice the onion and de-seed and chop the red pepper. Soften the onion in the oil over a gentle heat, pull the pan off the heat and add the paprika. Stir, add the red pepper and return to the heat. Stir, add the vinegar, cover and simmer until the pepper is soft. Push the sauce through the finest disc of a mouli, season with salt and pepper generously and simmer for a further 5 minutes uncovered. Transfer to a little pot and cool.

Chilli Sauce

2 fresh red chillis
2 tablespoons oil
2 hardboiled egg yolks
1 teaspoon tomato purée
1 tablespoon strong stock or
　consommé
seasoning

De-seed the chillis and soften in 1 teaspoon of the oil over a gentle heat. Push the egg yolk with the softened chillis through a fine sieve into a bowl. Add the tomato purée and the oil very slowly, beating with a wooden spoon all the time until you have a creamy consistency. Thin down with the consommé as needed. Taste, adjust seasoning.

Tomato and Marjoram Sauce

As this sauce is so useful in many dishes and will keep well with a layer of oil over the top and refrigerated, I am giving the most convenient quantities, which will, of course, yield more sauce than you need for the fondue.

1 14oz/396 g can of tomatoes
   (Italian plum tomatoes are the
   best for this sauce)
1 tablespoon oil
1 or 2 large cloves of garlic
a few sprigs of fresh marjoram

Push the tomatoes through a mouli to deseed. Heat the oil and slightly colour the whole garlic, then add the tomatoes, bring to simmering point and cook uncovered until reduced to at least half the quantity. Add the marjoram and season with salt and plenty of pepper. Simmer for a further 5 minutes.

Garlic Sauce

This garlic sauce is made with tahini (sesame paste) so it's not a true garlic sauce as such; nevertheless, it is excellent for a fondue.

1 or 2 juicy cloves of garlic
salt to taste
1 tablespoon tahini
the juice of ½ lemon
water to thin if necessary
1 dessertspoon olive oil

Crush the garlic with a little salt, using a pestle and mortar until it is quite liquid. Then combine it with the tahini, adding the lemon juice and a little water. Keep stirring until it goes white and is free of lumps, add more water if necessary. 'Finish off' the sauce with the oil.

Dill Sauce

1 hard-boiled egg yolk
1 teaspoon mild French mustard
1 teaspoon dill weed
½ teaspoon sugar
1 or 2 tablespoons olive oil

Mash the yolk with the mustard and dill weed, add the sugar, then incorporate the oil slowly. Correct the consistency by adding cream if it is too stiff. Taste and season; it should be slightly sweet and strongly flavoured with dill.

Moutarde à la Crème

Combine ⅓ strong Dijon mustard with ⅔ thick cream, season with salt and pepper and a little lemon juice. Whip slightly to give the sauce a foamy texture.

To serve, or rather present, a fondue, cube the meat into manageable bites and arrange it on the plates. It is hard to make piles of raw meat look either attractive or appetizing; a little garnishing with a sprig or two of any fresh herb can help a tiny bit but not much! Serve the sauces in individual ramekins or pots. It helps to bring the oil and butter up to temperature on the cooker before transferring it to its burner.

Note: When setting the table for a fondue it is wise to bear in mind that hot oil could possibly drip and damage an antique or highly polished table, so either use a thick table cloth or a large tray to stand the fondue on. Side or salad plates are essential. And do remember to take care when eating the fondue; it is very easy to burn your lips on a fondue fork that has just emerged from the boiling oil.

Jacket Potatoes

*2 or 4 potatoes depending on their
    size
oil
salt*

Scrub the potatoes well and rub
their skins with a little oil and
salt. Bake in a hot oven for
about 45 minutes.

Salade Niçoise

It may surprise you to know
that the true Salade Niçoise is
quite a simple salad, not a sort
of 'everything-thrown-in-plus
black olives' salad at all. It has
the great advantage of being
very suitable for making well in
advance.

*equal weights of cooked potatoes
    (waxy ones are best) and
French beans
oil
vinegar
salt and pepper
6 black olives
1 dessertspoon capers
6 or so anchovy fillets
some chopped chervil and tarragon if
    possible (if not you will have to
use either basil, marjoram or
oregano, but none of these are
really correct)
1 tomato for decoration*

Dice the potatoes and French
beans and mix them together
with some oil, vinegar, salt and
pepper to taste. Carefully mix
in the olives, capers and
anchovy fillets, making an
attractive arrangement with
the olives and perhaps one or
two of the anchovies. Slice the
tomato and decorate with the
slices. Sprinkle the chopped
herbs all over.

   If making this salad well in
advance, it is as well not to add
the tomato until the last minute
as it loses its freshness quickly
after being cut.

Avocado and Lime Chantilly

*1 avocado
juice of two fresh limes
2 teaspoons caster sugar
¼ pint/150 ml double cream
2 tablespoons soda water*

Peel the avocado, remove the
stone and dice it, sprinkle at
once with the juice of one lime
and one teaspoon of sugar.
Whip the cream until light and
frothy and add the remaining
lime juice and sugar. Whip a
little more and stir in the soda
water. Put the avocado in the
bottom of a tall glass and pour
the Chantilly cream on top.
Decorate with a twisted lemon
slice and chill.

   Serve with a langue de chat.
With a dessert like this it is a
pretty idea to place a small
freshly opened flower on the
top. It won't poison you and
you won't be tempted to eat it
anyway, but it will create an
artistic impression,
particularly if you match the
candles' colour to the flower.

A New Year's Eve Oblivionation

Morsels of Smoked and Cured Fish

Crêpes aux Epinards Surprise

Avocado and Melon Salad

Noisettes d'agneau en Croute
Courgettes in Rosemary Hollandaise
Small Jacket Potatoes with Thyme Butter

Cheese

Pink Champagne Cream

Why is it that when one is unhappy time almost stands still, just when one wants it to rush on? And when one is happy, really excitedly happy, time rushes by so fast one can hardly keep up with the pace it sets, just when one longs for it to stand still? Who or whatever ordered our lives has not got it quite right. Here is another paradox. None of us likes getting and looking older yet we do an awful lot of celebrating the fact. We celebrate birthdays, anniversaries and that most miserable marker of time, New Year's Eve. Why, I wonder, when most of us would rather forget that another year has gone? To celebrate is to observe, honour with rites, publish abroad, praise or extol and each of those definitions is the opposite of what I want to do to mark the fact that we are another year older!

Do not misunderstand me, I would not like to lose a single excuse for a dinner that is to be very special, but let me find another word to substitute for celebration. How about 'Oblivionation'? 'Would you like to come to my New Year's Eve Oblivionation?' meaning, of course, the sensational dinner I am going to cook not to remind me that yet another year has passed!

With a six-course menu such as this, the important factor to remember is that the portions must be very small and not rushed on one after another. Take it slowly, relax and savour every mouthful.

The choice of cheese is important; study the menu and consider what kind of cheese you think would compliment it as well as suit your taste. I would resist the temptation to buy a large selection. Just one really good cheese is much better and far more stylish.

I would serve a good chèvre on this occasion.

Morsels of Smoked and Cured Fish

These can be a mixture of bought and home cured. Hardly more than a mouthful of each one is needed. For example:

2 slivers of Gravad Lax (see page 82 for recipe)
2 small slices smoked eel (bought)
2 fillets (from one fish) smoked trout (bought)
2 portions lemon thyme and brandy-pickled carp

Lemon Thyme and Brandy-pickled Carp

1 fresh carp
2 tablespoons sugar
2 tablespoons coarse sea salt
a good fistful of fresh lemon thyme and common thyme chopped and mixed
3 tablespoons brandy
1 heaped teaspoon coarsely ground black pepper

Ask your fishmonger to bone the carp completely, removing the head and descaling at the same time, but leaving the skin on. Wash the fish, pat it dry, then go over it with your fingers and check there are absolutely no bones left in it at all. Mix all the pickling ingredients together. Choose a not too shallow dish the same size as the fish, spread one third of the mixture on the bottom of it and lay half of the fish on it, skin side down. Spread half the remaining pickling ingredients on the cut side of the fish and place the other half of the fish, skin side up, on top of it, spreading the remaining pickle over the skin. Cover with foil and place a heavy object (a brick perhaps) on top of it, and refrigerate for not less than 4 days, turning every day.

To serve, scrape off as much of the pickle as you can and cut thin strips across the grain – not the way smoked salmon is cut. Warm brown rolls should be offered, or brown toast.

Crêpes aux Epinards Surprise

2 tablespoons cooked chopped spinach
a few drops of lemon juice
coarsely ground black pepper
2 oz/50 g Roquefort cheese
2 very thin pancakes
1 oz/25 g butter

Squeeze as much liquid out of the spinach as possible and season it with lemon and pepper. Spread it on the pancake but not too near the edges. Place a piece of Roquefort cheese on top of the spinach so that when you roll up the pancake the cheese will be in the centre. Place the pancakes seam side down in a small gratin dish, spread the butter on top, cover with a piece of greaseproof paper and heat through thoroughly either in the oven or under the grill. Serve hot.

Avocado and Melon Salad

This little salad is to refresh the palate before the main course.

1 small avocado
1 very small ogen melon or a slice of a similar variety
juice of one lemon
a few grains of sugar

Slice both fruits as thinly as you can and combine them in little glass dishes or wine glasses. Pour the lemon over at once and sprinkle the sugar. Chill.

Noisettes d'agneau en Croûte

I do not know many short cuts and I am not sure if I even approve of them, but there is one here that I always take. I use frozen puff pastry.

It is important to know if the person who is sharing this 'Oblivionation' with you likes lamb pink or well done because in this case it makes a consider-able difference to your cooking method and timetable. It is the difference between long and slow cooking and short, sharp and fast.

1 oz/25 g butter
2 noisettes of lamb (the butcher will do them for you — ask him to trim off as much fat as he possibly can)
1 tablespoon port
8 oz/225 g frozen puff pastry
egg mixed with a little milk or water for glaze

Heat the butter in a frying pan and sear the lamb on both sides to seal it thoroughly. Add the port to the lamb and cook for 30 seconds only. Remove from the heat and allow to cool completely – still in the pan. When the meat is cold, roll out the pastry as follows. Cut it in half and roll out 2 circles, each one being enough to envelop a noisette. It will need to be fairly thin to obtain the size, so handle with care. Place the lamb on one half of the circle of pastry, scrape some of the port and butter juices from the bottom of the pan and put on top of the lamb, season with a little salt and pepper. Fold over the pastry to form a half-moon-shaped parcel, moisten the edges of the pastry and seal them together, folding them upwards so there is no chance any juices could escape. Brush the pastry with egg wash.

For pink lamb: bake in a hot oven preheated to 425°F/ 220°C/Gas Mark 7 for approximately 15 minutes, then let it stand for 5 or 10 minutes before serving. If you have prepared the lamb parcels in advance and refrigerated them until needed, increase the cooking time to 20 or 25 minutes, watching that the pastry does not over-colour; if it shows signs of doing so, protect it with a piece of foil laid on top of it.

For well-done lamb: bake as above until the pastry is golden, then turn the oven down to 300°F/ 150°C/Gas Mark 2 and cook for 1 hour or less.

Courgettes in Rosemary Hollandaise

3 or 4 rosemary needles
½ teaspoon lemon juice
2 egg yolks
2 oz/50 g softened butter
white pepper and salt
12 oz/350 g courgettes

Using a pestle and mortar, crush the rosemary needles with a little salt and combine them in the top of a double boiler (over just off-the-boil water) with the lemon juice; when the juice has almost evaporated, add the egg yolks and a piece of the butter and beat quickly with a wire balloon whisk until the butter has melted. Then add another little bit of butter, keep stirring all the time and make sure the water never boils. The sauce will begin to thicken. Continue the process until all the butter, little by little, has been incorporated, then remove from the heat and beat vigorously for 2 minutes, return to the heat and adjust seasoning. Keep warm over the hot water, ready to pour over the courgettes when you have cooked them as follows.

Unless they are very small, slit them in half lengthways and scoop out the seed pulp with a teaspoon, slice them so as to produce crescent-shaped ½-inch/1-centimetre thick bits. Steam them until just cooked, with still plenty of bite, then tip them into a hot serving dish and pour the rosemary hollandaise over. Serve hot or tepid.

Small Jacket Potatoes with Thyme Butter

a good size sprig of thyme
¼ teaspoon salt
3 oz/75 g unsalted butter
2 or 4 potatoes depending on their size

With a pestle and mortar crush the thyme with the salt very thoroughly, remove all bits of woody stalk, and combine it with the butter. Divide the butter in half and form pats. Chill. Bake the potatoes, after having rubbed their skins with a little oil and salt, in the usual way. Serve with the butter.

Pink Champagne Cream

This is wildly extravagant as it is exactly what its name implies – Pink Champagne incorporated into cream with a touch of Grand Marnier added. (Of course, you could use ordinary champagne with a dash of Augostura bitters if pink proved to be too difficult to find.)

6 fl. oz/175 ml double cream
scant 4 fl. oz/100 ml pink champagne
1 tablespoon Grand Marnier

Lightly whip the cream until it begins to thicken then, while still whipping, pour in – not too fast – the champagne and Grand Marnier. Continue to whip until you have a light fluffy consistency that will hold its form when piled into champagne glasses. Chill. Serve with a langue de chat.

After the Theatre

*Sliced Beef with Stilton,
Port and Horseradish Sauce
The Season's Vegetables au Nature*

Mousse de Café au Lait

The next three menus are designed for preparing well ahead of time, for example before going to the theatre, so that on returning it is all ready except for the very minimum of work, which is unavoidable if you are not going to serve a completely cold meal. In these circumstances I think it is reasonable to dispense with a first course in the strict sense of the word. Just concentrate on one rather good course. With one exception – where the main course is cold.

This meal requires almost completely cooking beforehand, leaving only the reheating of the dishes while at the same time putting the finishing touches.

Sliced Beef with Stilton, Port and Horseradish Sauce

The Bull House in Lewes, Sussex is now a restaurant, but it is also well-known for being the house in which Tom Paine lived from 1771 to 1779 before he returned to what were then still the American colonies. It was in this building, still little changed since Tom Paine's day, that I first enjoyed this dish created by Peter Adlam, who subsequently gave me the recipe.

1 teaspoon flour
1 teaspoon butter
approx. ¼ pint/50 ml consommé
1 oz/25 g Stilton
1½ oz/40 g freshly grated
  horseradish
1 oz/25 g butter (for frying)
4 3 oz/75 g slices of sirloin
2 tablespoons port
2 scant tablespoons double cream

Start by making the basis for the sauce. Make a roux with the flour and butter, then stir in the consommé until you have a pouring consistency. Add the Stilton and horseradish, stir well, then allow it to cool. When it has, liquidize and set aside for later use. Melt the butter in a heavy frying pan, seal the slices of meat on both sides, then quickly remove them from the pan and set aside. Add the port and the sauce to the butter left in the frying pan, stir well and turn off the heat until you return from the theatre. Then quickly bring to simmering point (that should take hardly a minute) and pop in the slices of sirloin. Turn them continuously for about 1 or 2 minutes and transfer them to a serving dish which you have warmed. Stir the cream into the sauce, bring to almost boiling point, pour at once over the meat and serve.

The Vegetables

The secret here is to cook your vegetables almost to the point of readiness to serve and at once refresh them in cold water. Then do the reverse to reheat them when needed – that is plunge them into fast-boiling water for 1 minute, drain and transfer to a heated serving dish and pour bubbling hot lemon and herb-flavoured butter over. If you have small metal steaming baskets and a very large saucepan of boiling water it is possible to reheat several vegetables at once to this standard of perfection, a highly desirable thing to be able to do at any time. Most vegetables respond well to this treatment, but of course there are a few obvious exceptions, like any finely chopped or creamed vegetable.

Mousse de Café au Lait

This is a very delicate and subtly flavoured mousse. It is not difficult to make, but it needs a gentle hand and patience. Do not make it too early in the day as it does not improve with keeping.

¼ pint/150 ml single cream
2 oz/50 g fresh high-roast coffee
  beans
¼ pint/150 ml double cream
2 tablespoons Perrier water
1 dessertspoon orange-flower water
¼ teaspoon caster sugar
2 egg whites

Tip the single cream into a saucepan, add the coffee beans (yes, it does seem an awful lot of beans!), bring just to the boil and take off the direct heat. Keep the cream and beans very warm for about 1½ hours, over a very low diffused heat or in a bain-marie, by which time it will have thickened. Cool. When cold, add the double cream to the coffee beans. Stir gently, watching very carefully because sometimes the cream thickens almost at once. Pour it through a strainer into a bowl. Because a lot of cream adheres to the beans it is now necessary to tip them back into the saucepan and add to them the Perrier water and orange-flower water. Stir well and strain into the cream, adding ¼ teaspoon of sugar or more to taste. With a wire balloon whisk whip the cream mixture until it thickens enough to be still mobile but not really pourable. Watch very carefully while doing this as it can curdle if overwhipped. Whisk the egg whites until they just hold their form and are greatly increased in volume but definitely not dry, and blend them into the cream thoroughly. Spoon into tall delicate white-wine glasses and chill.

Note: There is an alternative method with an alternative result using these ingredients. Turn it into a light and fluffy ice cream by freezing it either in an ice cream machine or in a bowl in the freezer or freezing compartment of the refrigerator. There is no need to whisk it while freezing, although it won't harm it to do so. Be sure to thaw slightly before serving.

After the Show

Pollo Picante
Okra with Brown Kidney Beans
Zucchini, Peppers, Tomato and Lime Pickle

Mango and Peach Salad

This meal is fairly highly spiced, being influenced by a combination of the Indian and Italian kitchens. It is well suited to serve after a show because every dish is improved by being cooked in advance and reheated later. I am not quite sure why that should be, unless it has to do with the spices; I only know from experience that it is so.

If you have any worries about serving such a highly spiced meal late in the evening, I suggest you offer a beautiful and aromatic cup of fennel tea to round off the meal. This delicious and naturally gentle digestive has a delicate flavour quite in keeping with the mood of the meal.

Pollo Picante

(spiced chicken)

2 drumsticks
2 boned breasts of chicken
½ teaspoon coarsely ground cinnamon
¼ pint/150 ml yogurt
1 white onion
1 or 2 fresh chillis
1 dessertspoon oil
1 teaspoon cumin seed
1 dessertspoon sweet paprika
1 clove of garlic
a pinch of finely grated lemon rind
1 small red pepper, finely chopped
1 level dessertspoon cornflour
1 tablespoon strong chicken stock

Skin the drumstick and cube the breasts. Rub them well with the cinnamon and marinate them in the yogurt for an hour. Finely chop the onion and chillis, having first removed their seeds. Heat the oil in a flameproof earthenware or terracotta casserole and gently soften the onion and chillis. Add the cumin seed, paprika and chopped garlic; strain the chicken, retaining the yogurt, and also add it. Stir to coat the chicken, then add the stock, lemon rind, red pepper and half the yogurt. Cover and simmer very slowly for about 45 minutes. Combine the remaining yogurt with the cornflour and stir it into the chicken. Season to taste. Now set it aside until you want to serve it, then bring it to simmering point for a minute or two, stirring gently.

You may feel you need to serve rice with this dish; that is quite all right so long as it is plain rice.

Okra with Brown Kidney Beans

2 cloves of garlic
1 tablespoon oil
1 teaspoon black mustard seed
4 large fresh green chillis
8 oz/225 g fresh okra
a small cooked potato
½ a can of Italian brown kidney beans
1 dessertspoon tomato purée
1 dessertspoon apricot chutney and
1 of mango chutney
1 dessertspoon vinegar
salt

A flameproof earthenware dish is best for this too. If you do not have one, use a heavy based pan. Lightly brown the garlic in the oil, then add the mustard seed. De-seed the chillis and slice them into thin strips, add them to the garlic and mustard seed and gently fry them. Wash and trim the okra, being careful not to trim the stalk too close to the pod which could cause it to open during cooking – not a good thing aesthetically. Cook the okra for approximately 8 minutes in fast-boiling salted water, drain, refresh under cold water and set aside. Cube the potato and drain the beans, then combine in the saucepan with the okra and chillis. Bring to simmering point and finally add the tomato purée, chutneys and vinegar. Simmer for a further 4 minutes. It is now ready to serve hot (re-heated), cold (delicious!) or tepid (best of all).

Zucchini, Peppers, Tomato and Lime Pickle

This dish cooks so quickly you could actually do the preparations up to cooking point in advance and cook it at the last minute.

equal quantities of tomatoes,
*   zucchini (courgettes) and peppers*
*   – probably one of each is ample*
1 teaspoon oil
approx. 1 tablespoon of mild lime
*   pickle, the flesh of the lime*
*   chopped*

Peel the tomato. Slice the zucchini in half lengthways and remove the seed pulp. Remove the seeds from the pepper. Slice all the vegetables as finely as you can. Heat the oil, lightly sauté the vegetables without adding salt. After about 2 minutes add the lime pickle, stir and serve as soon as the zucchini have softened but still have a bite.

Mango and Peach Salad

A delicious combination of fruits my mother introduced me to, very simple and slightly exotic, highly delightful.

If you can find fresh fruits, wonderful; if not, canned mangoes with fresh peaches are fine, but I'm not too keen on canned both!

Slice the fruits decoratively and evenly and combine, pouring just a little freshly squeezed orange juice over. No cream. A little liqueur if you like. They look great when served in tall thin white-wine glasses. You could frost a sprig of mint and stick it in the top to give it an air of . . . je ne sais quoi!

Note: Having prepared this meal well in advance, I would also suggest you set the table before you go out, bearing in mind that flowers wilt quickly in very warm places unless they are very fresh, and that overhead lighting is unflattering and not very romantic. Put the flowers in a cool place till the last minute and be sure to use candles – they really are so flattering, warming, soothing and, dare I say it, romantic.

Opposite: *Spoil Her*

Overleaf left: *A New Year's Eve Oblivionation*

Overleaf right: *Happy Birthday, Darling!*

After the Opera

Stilton and Chive Soufflé

Gravad Lax
Salad of Cucumber and Watercress

Tarte aux Poires

This is, for me, potentially the most romantic evening, because I love the opera best of all forms of entertainment and I also adore Gravad Lax. I find it one of the most luxurious of foods with supreme flavour and texture. Try it anyway and see if you agree with me. If you don't, at least you'll understand me a little!

Gravad Lax is pickled salmon and I advise five days of pickling (although a shorter period of time is permissible). So you can see that this menu cannot be cooked on the spur-of-the-moment. Everything can be prepared in advance, leaving only the final cooking of the soufflé.

Stilton and Chive Soufflé

It may surprise you to know that the soufflé is ideal for serving when you want little to do at the last minute, and yet it always seems to imply a degree of skill and cleverness not obtainable by many. Let's keep it that way then – join the few!

½ oz/15 g butter
½ oz/15 g flour
*4 tablespoons milk heated to just
    under boiling point*
the juice of ¼ lemon
salt and lots of black pepper
3 egg yolks
5 egg whites
3 oz/75 g grated Stilton
15 chives scissored into small bits

Melt the butter and blend in the flour, cook for a minute or two then pour in the milk slowly while stirring, add the lemon juice, salt and pepper. Pull off the heat and add the egg yolks one at a time, alternating with the cheese and chives, stirring vigorously all the while. Cover and set aside until you return from the opera. Leave the egg whites in a bowl out of the fridge ready to whisk. Butter the soufflé dish.

All you have to do now is heat the oven to 375°F/190°C/Gas Mark 5. Whisk the egg whites till stiff and carefully but thoroughly fold them into the egg and cheese mixture, using a metal spoon to do so. Tip it into the soufflé dish, stand in a bain-marie and cook on the middle shelf in the oven for approximately 20 minutes. A good soufflé should be runny but hot in the very centre and set on the outer edge. If it is firm all the way through it is overdone and loses some of its magic. Of course, it will sink as soon as it comes out for serving, but it's meant to!

Gravad Lax

It is not very practical to make less than two pounds of this.

*2 lb/900 g tailpiece of fresh salmon
    boned but with skin left on*
1½ tablespoons coarse sea salt
*1½ teaspoons crushed or very coarsely
    ground peppercorns*
1½ tablespoons granulated sugar
*2 heaped tablespoons fresh dill
    chopped, if available – if not, 1½
    level tablespoons dried*
2 tablespoons of acquavite or brandy

Not less than 48 hours but preferably 5 days before you are planning to serve this meal, prepare the Gravad Lax. Make quite certain there are no bones left in the salmon, wash it and dry it. Combine all the pickling ingredients together, spread a third on the bottom of a flat dish, lay a piece of salmon skin side down on top of it, spread the cut side with half of the remaining pickle, cover with the other piece of salmon skin side up and spread the remaining pickle on top. Cover with foil, press down with a heavy object and leave in the fridge for the necessary time, turning the fish daily.

To serve, scrape off the pickle and carve as you would smoked salmon (do this while the soufflé is in the oven). It is traditional in Scandinavia and, I think, an awful mistake, to serve an overbearingly strong dill sauce with Gravad Lax. Please don't do it. Just serve it as it is with hot brown rolls and this delicate salad with its hint of dill in it.

Salad of Cucumber and Watercress

This can be prepared before you go out and put undressed in the least cold part of the fridge.

a small cucumber
a small part of an iceberg lettuce
1 large bunch of watercress
leave no store unturned to find fresh dill —failing that, a good pinch of dried
the juice of ½ a lemon
a tablespoon of olive oil and very, very mild French mustard mixed together
½ teaspoon caster sugar
a little salt and pepper

Peel and chop the cucumber by hand into tiny pieces. Slice the lettuce very small with a sharp knife – do not tear it. Do likewise with the watercress and fresh dill (if you have it). Combine in a glass serving bowl. When you are ready to bring it to table sprinkle the dressing ingredients over one at a time and toss.

Tarte aux Poires

This takes a little time to make, but can certainly be done a day ahead. Take your time because a rushed job will not be very satisfactory.

For the pastry
see the recipe for Pâte Sucrée on page 31 and bake blind.

For the filling
2 cooking apples
½ oz/15 g butter
1½ oz/40 g sugar
1 tablespoon Poire Williams (liqueur)
2 conference pears
lemon juice
2 tablespoons apricot jam for glaze

Roll out the pastry and line an 8-inch/20 centimetre flan tin which you have greased. To bake blind prick the bottom all over with a fork, cover the pastry with foil and fill with beans or such to weight it down. Bake in a preheated oven 375°F/190°C/Gas Mark 5 until the pastry is a very pale gold. Remove the foil for the last 3 or 4 minutes. Cool.

Peel, core and coarsely chop the apples. Melt the butter in a stainless-steel saucepan, add the apples and cook very slowly. When soft, beat with a wooden spoon, bring to the boil and add the sugar. Boil until slightly thickened, stirring most of the time. Pull off the heat and, when cool, stir in the Poire Williams. If it is not completely smooth, push through a sieve. Peel and core the pears, slice them as thinly and evenly as possible, sprinkling with lemon juice to prevent discoloration (it helps if the pears are slightly under-ripe). Spread the apple purée in the flan case, then arrange the pear slices overlapping in an ever-decreasing circle. Bake in the oven at 375°F/190°C/Gas Mark 5 briefly to soften and slightly cook the pears. To make the apricot glaze put the jam in a saucepan and heat it; when it has melted strain it and return it to the pan. Add a spoonful or two of water and boil until you have a syrup-like consistency. Turn the tarte out of the flan tin on to a serving dish and paint on the glaze while it is still warm. Serve tepid with lightly whipped cream.

Fondue Affair

Fondue de Pêcheur
Tomato Salad Pistou

Monte Bianco

There is enormous scope with this fondue because there are so many suitable fish, but it is of the utmost importance that the fish should be fresh, really fresh. That is not to say it can never be frozen; for example, swordfish, which is wonderful to fondue, often has to be frozen to reach us. But, where possible, use today's catch! I have suggested various suitable fish, but you can choose any you fancy. Bear in mind that there must not be any bones – this is vitally important. Cut the fish into bite-size bits and keep them on a plate of ice until they are needed. In this way you will avoid a fishy smell, which can be off-putting. You can use half oil and half butter for the fondue, but if you felt inclined to use clarified butter it would be even better, albeit extravagant.

The fish

4 scallops
a tail piece of monkfish (known as
    goosefish in America)
1 large swordfish steak
4 king-size prawns

The sauces

Vinaigrette Sauce
a free adaptation

1 small tomato peeled and deseeded
    leaving only the flesh
½ teaspoon mustard, French or
    English
½ teaspoon salt
plenty of pepper
1 tablespoon tarragon or wine
    vinegar
2 tablespoons olive oil
a pinch of sugar

Push the tomato flesh through
a sieve to purée it. Stir the
mustard, salt and pepper into it
and beat it well. Then add the
vinegar and finally the oil, beat
vigorously, taste and adjust
seasoning with sugar.

Tartare Sauce

approximately 2 tablespoons basic
    mayonnaise
1 teaspoon capers chopped
2 or 3 gherkins chopped
½ teaspoon freshly grated
    horseradish
1 spring onion
1 teaspoon chopped parsley
1 dessertspoon cream

Mix all ingredients well
together and turn into little
saucepots.

Raw Chilli Sauce (very hot)

3 red chillis
½ red pepper
1 tablespoon capers
1 teaspoon salt
1 tablespoon sweetish sherry
a pinch or two of sugar
a few drops of lemon juice
1 teaspoon chopped parsley

Meticulously de-seed the chillis
and chop them very, very
finely; do the same with the
pepper. Chop the capers and
add them to the chillis and
peppers, mix well together,
adding the salt, cover and leave
to stand for 20 minutes. Then
add the sherry, sugar and

lemon juice, mix and add the
parsley, cover and leave to
stand for 1 hour at room
temperature. If you find the
sauce too hot to bear (having
been fair to it and tasted it not
on its own but with a piece of
cheese), then combine it with
thick yogurt, and serve.

Tomato and Anchovy Sauce

Make the tomato sauce as
described on page 67, and add
4 pounded anchovy fillets while
the required amount of sauce is
still hot.

Garlic and Parsley Sauce

2 fat cloves of garlic
1 tablespoon olive oil
salt and pepper
1 bunch of fresh parsley
2 oz/50 g butter
a few drops of lemon juice

If you have a blender or food
processor there is a very easy
and quick way to make this
sauce. Peel the garlic and fry it
in the oil just long enough for it
to begin very slightly to colour,
then remove it from the heat at
once. Chop the parsley roughly

(including the stalks, as they hold the most flavour), and with the garlic and butter process it until smooth, then add the hot oil, salt, pepper and a few drops of lemon juice, process to combine.

To do this by hand, first chop the parsley and lightly fried garlic very finely, then cream the butter and add it, combining all the other ingredients while whisking with a fork.

Serve in little pots which you have first warmed.

Tomato Salad Pistou

4 firm ripe salad tomatoes
12 fresh basil leaves
1 fat clove of garlic
3 Brazil nuts, ground
1 teaspoon parmesan cheese
3 or 4 tablespoons olive oil
2 teaspoons vinegar or lemon juice
salt and pepper to taste

Peel and de-seed the tomatoes, which is made easier by plunging the tomatoes in and out of boiling water. Chop the tomatoes into small chunks and put them in a serving bowl. Using a pestle and mortar, pound the basil leaves with the garlic and a little salt. When they are reduced to liquid, add the ground Brazil nuts and parmesan, then mix in the olive oil and vinegar, taste and adjust seasoning. Pour over the tomatoes and serve at room temperature – do not put it in the refrigerator.

Monte Bianco

This is the Italian recipe for Mont Blanc! I learned the Italian way so that is the method I must pass on to you.

12 oz/350 g chestnuts
milk
2 tablespoons Marsala or brandy
1 tablespoon caster sugar
¼ pint/150 ml cream

Make a definite split in the top (pointed end) of each nut and put in a pan of cold water. Bring to the boil, remove from the heat and peel the chestnuts, removing the inner skin as well.

Place the peeled chestnuts in a pan and cover with milk, simmer until they are quite tender. Drain them and push them through the finest disc of a mouli. Stir in the Marsala or brandy, sugar and 1 tablespoon of cream and mix well. Change the disc on the mouli to the medium size then, holding the mouli steady over the serving dish, push the chestnuts through a second time, allowing the vermicelli-like strands to pile up. Chill. Very slightly whip the cream so it thickens but can still be poured and decorate the pile of chestnut purée with it prior to serving.

Christmas Eve Supper

*Goujons of Trout
with a Delicate Sauce*

*Terrine of Pheasant
French Bread*

A Turinois

As you will probably be enjoying traditional Christmas fare tomorrow, Christmas Eve calls for something light and easy and a little festive maybe. And perhaps it would be nice to be able to put it on a tray and take it to the fireside to eat with the fingers while you put the last-minute touches to the Christmas tree, or do the final wrapping of presents.

Only the fish need last-minute attention. Everything else is prepared well in advance. The terrine can be made two or three weeks ahead and certainly should have been made not less than a week before needed, and kept in the fridge. You can prepare the fish up to deep frying point in the morning if you wish.

Goujons of Trout with a Delicate Sauce

2 small trout, filleted and skinned
seasoned flour
1 egg beaten with a teaspoon of oil
crushed cornflakes
oil for deep frying

For the sauce
1 teaspoon very mild French mustard
1 egg yolk
½ teaspoon dill weed
½ teaspoon caster sugar
½ teaspoon tomato purée
a pinch of salt
a drop or two of lemon juice
olive oil and sunflower oil mixed (or
*   a very mild light olive oil)*

Prepare the sauce first. Combine all the ingredients except the oil and beat vigorously. Add the oil as you would for mayonnaise, very very slowly, a drop at a time to begin with, then a little faster, until you have a creamy consistency. Taste and adjust seasoning if necessary.

Prepare the trout as follows: slice each fillet into strips lengthways, then halve the strips. You should end up with little pieces of fish the size of your little finger (if it is a thinnish one); in other words, you will have little fish fingers! Roll them in the flour, egg and cornflake crumbs. Do this with care, one at a time, making sure they are completely coated. Keep in the fridge until you are ready to deep fry them. Deep fry in the same way as you would chips, until golden and crisp, not too many at one time though. Allow to drain on absorbent paper, keeping warm.

Serve with the sauce to dip them in. A fondue fork is quite a handy thing to eat them with if you do not wish to use your fingers and are not intending to sit formally at table.

Pheasant Terrine

If you have recently cooked the breast of pheasant recipe on page 13 you will have enough pheasant meat for this terrine.

8 oz/250 g slightly cooked boned
*   gamey pheasant meat (from the*
*   leg and thigh is ideal and being*
*   slightly cooked makes it easier to*
*   remove from the bone)*
8 oz/225 g fairly lean pork
4 oz/100 g pure bacon fat cut in one
*   thick chunk*
1 dried pear
the liver of the pheasant if you
*   happen to have it*
6 juniper berries soaked in gin for 30
*   minutes*
6 peppercorns
1 bay leaf
4 tablespoons good-quality red wine
1 teaspoon coarse salt

Cut the pheasant meat into very small bits, making sure there is no shot or fragments of bone – often found after the splintering of a bone by shot. Mince the pork and cube the bacon fat fairly small. Cut the dried pear into strips like match sticks. Chop the liver. Combine all the ingredients together in a bowl and knead them with your hands. Put a cloth over the bowl and leave it to stand at room temperature for at least 1 hour. Fill an earthenware terrine with the mixture, pressing it well down. Put a greased piece of greaseproof paper over the top and put a lid on, place in a bain-marie in a preheated oven 325°F/160°C/Gas Mark 3 for approximately 1 hour. Allow to cool without opening. When cold, remove the greaseproof paper and replace it with pure lard melted and poured over the top – that way the terrine will keep for a month unopened in the refrigerator.

A Turinois

This, for me, is compulsive eating, so if I were following this recipe I would double the quantities to allow me to eat the leftovers secretly, if indeed there were any!

1 lb/450 g chestnuts
2½ oz/65 g of caster sugar
2½ oz/65 g unsalted butter
4 oz/100 g Menier chocolate
1 dessertspoon Grand Marnier

Peel the chestnuts of both their outer shell and inner skins, a tedious job but worth it in the end. There are a number of ways to get the skins off chestnuts; one is to make a cut in each nut and place them in a hot oven for a minute or two, then peel them. Another way is to put them in cold water, bring it to the boil, remove it from the heat and take the nuts out one at a time to peel. Either way it's painful! Steam the peeled chestnuts until they are cooked through and tender. Push them through the finest disc of a mouli or a sieve.

Cream the butter and sugar until quite white and creamy. Melt the chocolate with 2 tablespoons of water or coffee and when cool combine it with creamed butter and sugar into the sieved chestnuts. Add the Grand Marnier. Lightly oil a flan or cake tin and line the bottom with non-stick vegetable parchment and turn the mixture into it, smooth the surface and chill overnight. To serve, turn out and slice in wedges, offering whipped cream with it.

Happy Birthday, Darling!

Chilled Zucchini Soup

Fillet Steak 'As You Like It'
with Mustard Hollandaise and
Horseradish Hollandaise

Cabbage Hearts
Glazed New Potatoes

A Special Birthday Gâteau

And what better way of saying it is there than with thoughtfully and lovingly prepared food? None, in my opinion. Think of the compliment we are paying, the love we are lavishing because with every detail of the cooking, the person for whom we are doing it is always in mind, their pleasure and delight are uppermost in our thoughts. How can we make sure 'they' fully appreciate that fact? We cannot, but just know that if they are worth the trouble we are taking they will be aware of it without out having to say a word!

Chilled Zucchini Soup

This soup is made with spinach and zucchini (no different from courgettes; what I call them just depends on what mood I am in!)

4 oz/100 g spinach or chard
including stalks
1 courgette
1 teaspoon olive oil
½ pint/300 ml chicken or veal stock
1 small potato, finely grated
4 tablespoons white wine
½ oz/15 g fresh or frozen, but not
dried, basil
salt, pepper and nutmeg
cream for garnish

Coarsely chop the spinach and courgette, heat the oil in a saucepan and add them to it. Stir until slightly softened, then add the stock. Bring to the boil then add the potato. Cover and simmer until all the vegetables are soft, then add the wine. Bring back to boiling point and remove from the heat. Liquidize, and at the same time add the fresh or frozen basil. Strain through a fine sieve.

Season with salt, pepper and plenty of nutmeg. Chill.

When serving, place a spoonful of cream in the centre of each portion and float a tiny growing tip of basil on the top.

Fillet Steak 'As You Like It'

This is exactly what it says – rare, medium or well done! Two thin slices each, topped with a different sauce.

approx. 12 oz/350 g fillet steak cut
into 4 slices
clarified butter for frying

Mustard and Horseradish Hollandaise

4 tablespoons hollandaise sauce as
given on page 74, but omitting
the rosemary
1 scant teaspoon strong Dijon
mustard
1 scant teaspoon grated horseradish

Prepare the sauces by combining the mustard with 2 tablespoons of hollandaise and the horseradish with the other 2 tablespoons, keeping them warm in separate containers over hot but not boiling water. The meat must be cooked at the very last minute – not even just before you sit down: it must be after you have finished the first course. But only takes seconds to cook if you have everything prepared and waiting. It is important to remove every piece of fat and sinew and trim the steaks to nice even rounds. Melt plenty of clarified butter in a very large frying pan and have it warm and ready to bring quickly to a fierce heat. Have the sauces and warm plates to hand. Having found out whether it is to be rare, medium or well done, fry the steaks on both sides accordingly. If one of you likes your steak well done and the other rare, put the steaks to be rare in the pan just before the other two have completed cooking so they all come out of the pan together for simultaneous serving, which is desirable whenever possible. Put a dollop of each sauce on top of the steaks – and serve.

Cabbage Hearts

If it is the time of the year when the primo cabbage is on the market that is the one to go for. It has a wonderful flavour and the heart is soft and not too compact. If primo is not available then any fairly loose-forming cabbage will do. Not white cabbage which does not seem to have a heart – possibly because it is all heart!

Remove the tough outer leaves of the cabbage, trim the stalk but not too much otherwise the cabbage will fall apart. Quarter it and simply steam it until it is very lightly cooked, then sprinkle with lemon, fennel seed or feathers and butter. It will stand being kept warm over simmering water in its serving dish for a short while.

Glazed New Potatoes

New potatoes seem to be available from somewhere most of the year now – at a price maybe, but lovely for just such a special occasion. If the potatoes are of the type which, when scrubbed, have transparent skins, so much the better. Unless they are very smooth and pale scrape off the skins. Plunge them into plenty of fast-boiling water and cook until they are very nearly done, then quickly drain off the water, pop in a big sprig of any fresh herb you favour, a knob of butter and a teaspoon both of lemon juice and sugar. Replace the lid at once so they continue to cook in their own steam, and the flavour of the herb will permeate them. Jiggle the pan over a gentle heat for a minute or two to coat them with the butter, lemon and sugar. Keep warm until needed but not for too long (better to re-heat them).

A Special Birthday Gâteau

This is a very adaptable gâteau, and it is also very rewarding to make. It cannot be done in a hurry. First of all find out what is the favourite fruit of the person for whom you are making this cake. Let us hope it is something like strawberries or raspberries. It would be very tricky if the choice were rhubarb! The next thing to be done is the gathering and frosting of a few small flowers and sprays such as summer jasmine, tiny roses, primroses, polyanthus, lavender – it just depends what you can find and what the season is. Do not use flowers from bulbs. Frost them as follows. Lightly beat the white of an egg and paint carefully all over the flower, dredge with caster sugar and set in a warm place on non-stick vegetable parchment to dry. This can take quite a while, so allow a morning, but once properly dry the frosted flowers will keep until you need them.

The gâteau

3 large fresh eggs, separated
2 oz/50 g sugar
2 oz/50 g plain flour
3 tablespoons Cointreau or Grand
  Marnier

The filling

¼ pint/150 ml cream
8 oz/225 g double cream cheese
1 tablespoon icing sugar
1 tablespoon ground toasted
  hazelnuts
6 oz/175 g chosen fruit, shall we say
  raspberries

The icing

4 oz/100 g unsalted butter
8 oz/225 g icing sugar
a few drops of lemon juice

Butter and flour 2
8-inch/20-centimetre sandwich
tins, lining the bottoms with
non-stick vegetable
parchment. Cream the egg
yolks and sugar until very light
and creamy. Whip the egg
whites until really stiff, then
fold them in. Sift the flour twice
then carefully fold it in also.
Spread a quarter of the mixture
in each tin and bake in a
preheated oven 350°F/180°C/
Gas Mark 4 for about 10 to 15
minutes. Turn out on to a cold
flat surface and repeat with the
remaining mixture.

Place 1 of the sponge layers
on a plate and pour the
Cointreau over it. Leave it to
soak in completely. Whip the
cream and combine it with the
cream cheese, stir in the sugar.
Divide it into 3 portions. Mix 1
portion with the toasted
hazelnuts and 2 portions with
the raspberries. On a large
plate or cake board place 1
layer of sponge and spread it
with 1 portion of the cream
cheese and raspberries. Place
another layer of sponge on top,
then spread the cream cheese
and hazelnut mixture. Top this
with the sponge soaked in
Cointreau by carefully sliding
it off the plate into position.
Now finish off with the final
portion of cream cheese and
fruit topped with the last
sponge.

To make the butter icing,
cream the butter until it is very
pale and very creamy, then
begin to add the sifted icing
sugar very, very slowly; half
way through add the lemon
juice, then finish off and beat it
very vigorously. Ice the cake all
over, starting with the sides,
then decorate with the frosted
flowers and chill if you possibly
can – anyway put it in the
coolest place possible.

You must surely love very
much the lucky person you are
making this cake for!

Summer Starlit Suppers

We had climbed the mountain gently and not for too long. The sun was setting as we reached our destination, the ancient ruins of a castle overlooking the Mediterranean towards Turkey. That special sound made by the crickets in hot countries seemed to be getting louder as light faded. As the sun sets in Cyprus so rises an evening full of wonder and promise. The air was suddenly filled with the aroma of meat cooking over charcoal, the smoke from time to time holding the fragrance of herbs.

This was my first experience of a night-time picnic. For in Cyprus it would be unthinkable not to barbecue either fish or meat for a picnic. In popular public beauty spots there are often to be found purpose built barbecues for anyone to use. I was staying in Cyprus with an uncle at the time of its independence. We were a large party on that evening; it was one of the most romantic picnics I have ever had. Helped, of course, by the fact that I did not have to lift a finger.

Eating outside, no matter where, at any time, is special, but at night is is exceptionally delicious. Outside can be anywhere from a balcony to a beach, it does not matter, there is always a degree of excitement present, maybe a slight feeling of adventure even; otherwise dormant senses seem to be awakened and stimulated. It's just a little magical, isn't it?

Beach Barbecue

Lamb Souvlakia
French Bean Salad
Stuffed Potatoes
Barbecued Corn on the Cob

Fresh Fruit

Cooking outside needs to be a joint activity; it's more fun that way. But I have a picture in my mind, probably quite inaccurate, of man making fire, hunting meat (I know that bit is correct) or catching fish (not sure about that, I think maybe women caught fish) and cooking it. While woman sat and waited! Maybe she baked a little or even prepared some beans or shoots, but mainly she waited for man to provide her with the cooked meat and fish. How does that sound to you? Let him make the fire then, and at least watch and turn if necessary, baste of course, throw herbs on to the coals and, generally speaking, cook the meat you have prepared for this Starlit Supper.

Lamb Souvlakia

Souvlakia means that the meat is grilled on a skewer. In Cyprus, the skewer is often over a metre long and pushed on to it are chunks of lamb jointed in a most bizarre fashion compared to our style. It is quite impossible to tell what part of the animal one is eating, but this in no way hinders the enjoyment; there is nothing to beat it. I do not intend to try to imitate because it would not work. Instead, I have found that the little cuts of lamb known as noisettes make a simply heavenly souvlakia.

4 noisettes of lamb
lemon and olive oil
fresh rosemary

Steep the meat in lemon and oil – 2 parts lemon to 1 part oil with fresh rosemary sprigs mixed in it – for 1 hour before cooking. Rub garlic up and down the skewer and thread the meat on it. Push the skewer from one outside edge to the other, across the lamb rather than through the centre. Season with salt and lots of pepper. Make sure the fire is really hot before putting the meat over it. Keep turning the skewer. Throw a handful of rosemary in the fire from time to time; the smell wafting from it will be divine, as well as the flavour imparted to the meat. Do not offer any sauces, they will mask the exquisite flavour of the lamb cooked this way.

French Bean Salad

The advantage of salads like this is that they will not wilt or be less appetizing through being slightly warm, perhaps due to travelling or sultry weather.

12 oz/350 g French beans
2 or 3 sprigs of fresh basil or your
  favourite fresh herb
the juice of ½ lemon
1 tablespoon really good olive oil
salt and pepper

Wash and trim the stalks from the beans but do not cut them up. Bring plenty of slightly salted water to the boil and plunge the beans in, taste one after 5 minutes and judge whether to go on cooking for a further minute or two. The beans should definitely be undercooked when you drain the water off, because they will go on cooking in their own heat. Having drained off the water, very quickly throw in the fresh herb, lemon, oil and seasoning. Put the lid on fast and shake the pan to distribute the oil and lemon. Leave to stand thus until cooled. The perfume of the herb will have permeated the beans which will have absorbed the dressing to a certain extent.

Everything in this meal is delightfully simple to prepare and should not be shunned for that reason; so often the simplest methods are the best and they frequently get overlooked in an effort to be 'different' or 'clever', a mistake in my view.

A Real Picnic Hamper

Stuffed Potatoes
(reheated in the fire)

2 big potatoes
2 lamb's kidneys
a little milk
1 oz/25 g butter
salt and pepper
oil to rub on the potatoes

Scrub the potatoes and rub
them all over with oil and salt.
Bake at 350°F/180°C/Gas
Mark 4 for about 1½ hours.

Carefully remove the skin
(membrane) and core from the
kidneys and leave them whole.
Season them.

Cut a lid in the long side of
the three-quarters cooked
potatoes, being very careful not
to damage the skins, scoop out
the pulp and mix it with a little
milk and half of the butter,
season it well. Replace a third
of it and then pop a whole
kidney in and cover it with the
remaining pulp, mound it up a
little and replace the lid. Wrap
the potatoes tightly in foil and
put them in (or on) a grill over
the fire for about 25 minutes,
depending on how hot the fire

is. When serving, put the
remaining butter under each
lid.

Barbecued Corn on the Cob

The corn on the cob can be
cooked at any time, maybe to
start the meal, or to finish it off!
There is nothing to be done
except to remove the silky
strands, but keep the husk on.
Soak it in water and place it
over the coals (not in them!),
turn frequently. You can also
cook it without the husk on;
quite different to eat but just as
good.

Note: If you do not have a
barbecue and all the equip-
ment that seems to accompany
it, do not feel you have to rush
out and buy everything. All you
really need are some fairly long
skewers, a couple of cake-
cooling racks and maybe a
number of bricks. Charcoal is a
relatively easy to use and quick
fuel, but again not essential. If
you can find plenty of hard
wood, such as oak, and burn it
down to glowing embers, that
would be wonderful. Simply
dig a hole in the ground, be it
beach or lawn, and make your
fire in it. Place your bricks
either side of the fire, lay the
cake racks on top of them and
voilà – a barbecue.

Four Friends

A Real Picnic Hamper

Tranche de Baguette Farcie

Boned and Stuffed Poussin
offered with a Selection of Raw and
Very Lightly Cooked Vegetables
to enjoy with a Green Mayonnaise
and a Pink Mayonnaise

Tartelettes aux Fruits

One of the joys of a picnic as a child was that we were allowed to eat everything with our fingers – something that was strictly forbidden at table. Times and manners have changed, thank heavens, because I encourage my children to pick up the bones of a chicken or chop and enjoy

the choice morsels of meat nearest the bone. Nevertheless, the picnic is still more relaxed than a meal at table, although I try, not always successfully, to draw the line at getting up and going paddling or exploring with food in hand! I feel the food should allow for a certain amount of fingers only, and should encourage the away-from-convention-and-rules feeling of freedom, but it must never be without style.

Tranche de Baguette Farcie
(stuffed French bread)

½ teaspoon paprika
1 oz/25 g butter
2 oz/50 g cream cheese
6 fresh chives
4 anchovy fillets
a squeeze of lemon juice
12 inches/30 cm of French bread
12 thin slices of cucumber
12 peeled prawns
12 strips of red, green and yellow
    pepper, mixed

Work the paprika into the butter then combine it with the cream cheese. Scissor the chives as finely as you can into the cream cheese mixture. Mash the anchovies with the squeeze of lemon. Divide the bread into two 6-inch/15-centimetre lengths, cut a small slice off the top of the bread, thus exposing the soft inside, and carefully pull it all out, leaving a hollow, crusty shell rather like a boat. Put the soft bread on one side, you may be needing it for another recipe. Spread the mashed anchovies thinly over the inside bottom of the hollowed-out bread, then put in the cream cheese mixture. Stand a piece of cucumber on edge across the slice of bread and secure it upright by embedding it in the cream cheese; next put a prawn, then a piece of pepper, then cucumber and so on, 6 of each per slice of bread.

Boned and Stuffed Poussin
(Spring Chicken)

1 large clove of garlic
a few corriander seeds lightly
    crushed
a pinch of cumin seeds
scant ½ teaspoon allspice and
    paprika mixed
1 teaspoon lard
1 teaspoon cider vinegar
3 tablespoons dry cider
6 oz/175 g coarsely minced pork
2 oz/50 g minced beef
¼ teaspoon salt
8 tiny button mushrooms
pepper to taste
1 boned poussin

To bone a chicken you need a very sharp slender knife or a very nice butcher; I would plump for the latter! But should he be 'out of sorts' today, I will try to explain how to do it, as best as I can. Lay the cleaned and drawn bird on its breast. Cut through to the bone along the whole of its back. Cutting close to the bone, work off the flesh and skin together. Working towards the thigh ball and socket joint, sever the sinews there, loosen the flesh and pull the bone up, scraping the flesh downwards and thus turning the leg inside out. When the next joint is reached, cut the sinews and remove the bone. Treat the wings in the same way, having first removed the wing tips (pinions). Work around the breast bone with great care. It is important not to puncture the skin, which is very easy to do in this area. Remove the carcase and set aside for stock. It is well to remember that boning can be made impossible by the use of a blunt, thick knife; do not attempt it unless you have a really sharp, very thin, slightly flexible knife.

Lay the bird on its breast again, turn the legs and wings back the right way and tie the open ends, fold in the neck skin and stitch up the opening right down to the tail, leaving an opening to stuff through.

To make the stock, use the bones of the bird; onion and any root vegetable available; a bouquet of thyme, sage and marjoram covered in half and half water and cider. Season with plenty of salt and pepper and simmer for about 2 hours. Strain and reduce by half.

To make the stuffing, finely chop and fry the garlic with the spices very gently in the lard for a minute, then add the vinegar and cider, bring to the boil and take off the heat at once. Cool it. Combine the pork and beef mince together, adding the salt, pour the cooled spiced liquid over, mix well, and leave to stand for at least 2 hours (overnight would be better). Work the now well-flavoured meats with your hands to form a really compact mixture, adding a dessertspoon or two of the stock to it. Fill the bird, shaping it as you go. Thread the mushrooms on to a very thin skewer or knitting needle (anything fat or thick would split them). With your fingers make a tunnel in the centre of the stuffing in the bird and insert the mushrooms, pulling out the knitting needle and pressing a bit more stuffing in the end to encase them completely. Sew up the opening or secure it with wooden toothpicks.

Place the bird in an earthenware casserole and pour the stock over, cover and place in a preheated oven 450°F/ 230°C/Gas Mark 4 for 10 minutes, then turn the oven down to 300°F/150°C/Gas Mark 2 and cook for a further 45 minutes. Allow the bird to cool in the stock very slowly.

To serve, slice straight across the bird in thick slices, or halve it lengthways.

The Vegetables

Choose vegetables that are fresh and crisp; if packed in a cold box straight from having been soaked in iced water they should retain some bite. A selection of the following works well.

a lettuce heart
strips of cucumber
fresh white raw mushrooms
lightly cooked French beans and tiny
  courgettes
cold new potatoes cooked in their
  skins
lightly cooked calabrese
raw cauliflower broken into florets
spring onions (if you like them)
firm tomatoes

Green Mayonnaise

12 large basil leaves
½ teaspoon salt
1 teaspoon lemon juice
2 tablespoons thick basic mayonnaise
2 teaspoons cream

Pound the basil leaves to a pulp with the salt, adding the lemon juice when they are completely liquid; incorporate carefully into the thick basic mayonnaise. Fold in the cream.

Pink Mayonnaise

This may be flavoured with chilli or anchovy mixed with tomato purée and added to the basic mayonnaise, the choice is yours. Or simply add the tomato purée and a herb of your choice. The method is the same as above. Both sauces would look good in colourful pottery bowls. Use cling film to prevent spillage.

Tartelettes aux Fruits

For the pastry

Use either Pâte Sablée (see page 27) or Pâte Sucrée (see page 31)

For the filling

3 egg yolks
1 dessertspoon sugar
6 fl oz/175 ml cream
6 or 8 cooked tartelette cases
a small quantity of any or all of the
  following fruit:
  cherries, stoned
  redcurrants and whitecurrants
  seedless grapes
fraises des bois (best of all)
apricot glaze (see page 83)

Beat the egg yolks with the sugar until pale, smooth and creamy. Scald the cream and pour it over the eggs while stirring, place over simmering water and stir until well thickened. Cool and chill. Fill each tartelette case with this cold custard cream.
Completely cover the custard cream with the chosen fruit and glaze it with the thin apricot glaze. There is no need to sweeten the fruit as the pastry, cream and glaze are sweet; in fact, the tartness of any fruit is desirable.

Almost the Conclusion

Four Friends

Melitzanes Stifatho
Spiced Chicken Kebabs
Pork Afelia Kebabs
Cypriot Style Salad
Hot Pitta Bread

Watermelon Surprise

A candlelight dinner for two is a beautiful, civilized and fairly sophisticated way of communing with someone you may wish to know better or someone you have known and loved over the years. I think we should all do it more frequently; it surely must be one of the gentlest and least aggressive

ways of communicating. May I suggest now just one menu for four people for a sultry summer evening in the garden, by starlight and candle? Four romantically inclined people to share the magic and peace of night barbecuing.

Melitzanes Stifatho

I hesitate to give the literal translation because it sounds so unattractive in English, whereas the dish tastes wonderful. Aubergine Stew!

1½ lb/675 g aubergines
8 oz/225 g shallots
1 14oz (396 g) can of tomatoes
5 cloves of garlic
¼ pint/150 ml olive oil
2 tablespoons red wine vinegar
1 scant teaspoon honey
1 bay leaf
2 or 3 sprigs of basil
salt and pepper

Cut the aubergines into chunks and sprinkle generously with salt, leave them to drain for 1 hour. In Cyprus you would stand them in the sun to do this! Dry the aubergines thoroughly and, with the peeled but whole shallots and garlic, put them in a saucepan with all the other ingredients. Bring to boiling point, then simmer for 1 hour, stirring from time to time. Should it become too dry add a little water, but it should not be too liquid. Pull off the heat and leave to become tepid. Serve with thick chunks of bread spread with garlic butter and toasted over the barbecue.

Spiced Chicken Kebabs

1 teaspoon salt
1 bay leaf
2 cardamom seeds broken open
1 chilli split open
¼ teaspoon ground nutmeg
1 teaspoon green peppercorns
¼ teaspoon cinnamon
1¼ lb/575 g boned and skinned
 breast of chicken
3 tablespoons of lemon juice
3 tablespoons olive oil

Using a pestle and mortar, pound the salt with the bay leaf, cardamom seeds and a very small piece of chilli, combine it with the nutmeg, cinnamon and peppercorns. Cube the chicken and mix the spices into it with your hands, adding the rest of the chilli. Pour the lemon juice over, mix well, then pour the oil over. Leave to stand for about 2 hours, then thread on 2 long skewers. Baste with the marinade when cooking over very hot coals.

One skewer of each meat for each couple to share! Heat the pitta bread in seconds over the fire, split it open and let each person stuff their own if they wish. To be enjoyed with the following Cypriot salad.

Pork Afelia Kebabs

1¼ lb/575 g pork tenderloin
1 dessertspoon roughly crushed
  coriander
2 tablespoons olive oil
salt and pepper
enough red wine (Othello) to cover

Cube the pork in even pieces, not too small. Mix with the crushed (definitely not ground) coriander seed, oil, salt and pepper. Pour enough red wine over to cover it and leave as long as possible (for example, prepare this in the morning and cook it the same evening). Using 2 long skewers, thread the meat on and push it well together. The meat will be very tender. Baste it with the marinade while cooking over a hot bed of charcoal.

Cypriot Style Salad

1 very crisp lettuce or part of a white
  cabbage or Chinese leaves
1 large tomato
1 small onion
1 ridge cucumber
a few celery heart leaves
fresh coriander leaves if available
6 or 8 black olives
1 teaspoon of capers
4 to 6 oz/100 to 175 g feta cheese
  (from good delicatessens)
2 tablespoons good strong olive oil
a little lemon juice
salt and pepper

Shred the lettuce, cut up the tomato into chunks (the skin should not be tough at barbecuing time of the year), thinly slice the onion, cut the cucumber into chunks, combine all these ingredients in a salad bowl. Scissor the celery leaves and coriander over the top, sprinkle the capers over, drop in the olives and crumble in the cheese. Do not mix. Sprinkle with salt, pepper and lemon juice, and trickle the oil over. Still do not mix because it automatically gets mixed enough when being served.

Watermelon Surprise

This idea comes from someone with whom I have never had a candelelit dinner for two, though we have enjoyed many for four. He is my favourite tenor, David Rendall, whose voice I have often listened to while writing this book.

Cut a hole or two the size of a 10-pence piece in the top of the melon, carefully withdraw the piece of cut melon, pierce the flesh with a fat skewer a few times, then pour in port. Put the pieces of melon back. Ideally this should be done 2 days before and topped up from time to time.

   To serve, be crude just for once, cut it into large slices and thoroughly enjoy it!

A Fantasia

Should you ask me with whom I would most like to dine by candlelight, I would be torn between two musicians, Richard Strauss and Gioacchino Rossini. Richard Strauss fills me with breathtaking awe and I feel that I know him quite well; his music tells so much. I would fear the meeting and tremble at the thought of presenting a feast before the man who can reduce me to tears of wonder at sounds so beautiful depicting scenes sometimes so savage and horrific (Salome) that I feel a puppet in his hands. And yet to dine with him would be an excitement almost beyond enduring, for I admire and love his music, his skill and his artistry with so much fervour. But maybe I would lose my appetite! On the other hand, we all know something of Rossini's taste in food, and dishes known to have delighted him are still being served today. So choosing a menu for his delectation should not be so awesome. His genius, his zest for life, his love of the practical joke, his wonderful spontaneity and, above all, his tremendously vigorous and vibrant music appeal to me so much that I am sure it would be a very amusing as well as an immensely stimulating evening. Imagine picking up the napkin he used and finding a duet scribbled out on it, an idea which came to him while the dishes of one course were being exchanged for another! I would like to meet him just after he composed *La Pietra die Paragone* or perhaps *Mosé in Egitto*, when he was in his twenties. Yes, I think it has to be Rossini for dinner this time.

When planning a gastronomic menu with so many courses, it is important to remember that each course must be of a modest size, mere morsels of delectable delights to tickle and stimulate the palate while unobtrusively satisfying the hunger.

The Menu for Rossini

Crêpes Vertes au Fromage de Chèvre

Minted Cauliflower

Fillets of Mackerel cooked in Mustard Cream

Borsch Sorbet

Roast Grouse aux Noix
with Salad

A Mature Stilton

The English Treacle Tart

York Ham in Port Grilled in a Field Mushroom

Coffee

Crêpes Vertes au Fromage de Chèvre

The influence is a combination of Hungary and France, and the dish should be eaten very hot. It can be prepared in advance and heated through at the last minute.

1 egg
2 tablespoons flour
about 6 fl oz/175 ml milk
1 tablespoon of cooked and sieved spinach
salt
¼ teaspoon sugar
4 oz/100 g fromage de chèvre
butter

Work the egg into the flour with a fork, moisten with a little milk and add the spinach, salt and sugar, beat well, then add as much milk as you need to get a fairly thick pancake batter. (You will now have more batter than you need for this menu, but it is not practical to reduce the quantities any further, and pancakes freeze well.) For this recipe you will need 8 small circles of pancakes 3 inches/8 centimetres in diameter. These are best achieved by cutting them out of bigger pancakes, which need to be slightly thicker than usual in this case. Chèvre usually comes in cylindrical form about 2½ inches/5 centimetres in diameter. Cut 4 slices and sandwich them between the pancakes. Place a dollop of butter on top of each one and, just before serving, place under a very hot grill to heat through and soften the cheese. This could also be done in a very hot oven if more convenient.

Minted Cauliflower

The cauliflower has such a delicate and yet distinctive flavour that it is a beautiful vegetable to serve as a dish on its own; its texture in particular is so good, providing you are very mindful of exact cooking time.

1 very small head of cauliflower
1 large bunch of mint
½ lime
2 oz/50 g unsalted butter
just a pinch of sugar
salt

Trim the cauliflower, cutting off as much of the stalk as possible while still keeping the head whole. Line the bottom of your steamer with half of the washed fresh mint and set the cauliflower on it. Pack the remaining mint all round and on top of the vegetable. Bring the water to the boil and steam the cauliflower for about 5 minutes, but taste and adjust according to your liking, remembering that it must not be even well cooked; there must be a crispness in every mouthful. Halve the cauliflower and place in 2 individual serving dishes. Squeeze the lime. Melt the butter until it foams, sprinkle the lime juice over the cauliflower, along with the sugar and salt. Pour the foaming butter on, decorate with a sprig of fresh mint. It does not harm the dish to serve the vegetable merely warm or tepid providing you dress it with the lime and hot butter at the last minute.

Fillets of Mackerel in Mustard Cream

One fish should be enough if it is a reasonable size, and it is imperative that it is very fresh indeed; there is nothing worse than tired mackerel, the flavour is poor and the texture becomes cotton woolly.

1 heaped teaspoon strong Dijon mustard
2 fillets of mackerel
½ pint/300 ml double cream
1 tablespoon brandy
pepper coarsely ground and salt to taste

Spread the mustard all over the raw fillets, bring the cream to simmering point in a small frying pan and add the mustard-coated fish; bring back to the boil, add the brandy and simmer, turning the fish once or twice for a few minutes until just cooked. Season with salt and pepper and put aside until you are ready to serve. Then either reheat in the same pan over a gentle heat or put into individual dishes. A piece of warm French bread should be offered with it.

Borsch Sorbet

I find it very difficult to make ice cream just for two. Since it keeps well in a freezer and it is as much trouble to make enough for two as it is for eight, I recommend making the larger quantity, particularly as it is easier to handle.

½ oz gelatine
3 good-size freshly cooked beetroots
1 teaspoon dried dill weed or 1 dessertspoon finely chopped fresh dill
1 tablespoon wine vinegar
1 dessertspoon sugar
¼ pint/150 ml good clear stock

Dissolve the gelatine in 4 tablespoons of warm water. Purée the beetroot, making absolutely certain it is completely free from any lumps, and add the dill, vinegar and sugar. Heat the stock a little and combine it with the dissolved gelatine. Stir it into the puréed beetroot, season to taste and freeze as described on page 18.

Roast Grouse aux Noix

It is usual to serve one bird per person, but in these circumstances I think half a bird each would be quite sufficient.

It is important to make sure the grouse is a young one with pointed tips to the wings and a downy breast. Alas, I do not think you can do more than prepare the bird for cooking earlier in the day, cook it just before sitting at table and leave the sauce separate until you serve.

1 young grouse
1 lemon
2 tablespoons walnut oil
4 oz/100 g shelled walnuts
1 Golden Delicious apple
1 teaspoon honey
1 tablespoon cider vinegar
salt and pepper

Split the grouse along its backbone and open it up like a book; snip the sinews in the leg and thigh joints, run a skewer straight through the bird to keep it open and flat. Rub it with a little salt. Squeeze the lemon juice and pour it over the bird, rub it well in all over, then do likewise with 1 tablespoon of the walnut oil; set aside thus, in a shallow dish, to marinate for 1 hour or more. Heat the remaining oil in a large thick-bottomed frying pan and fry the grouse on both sides over a fairly fierce heat for about 6 minutes on each side, then reduce the heat and continue cooking and turning for a further 6 minutes approximately. Remove the bird from the pan and place on a hot serving dish to keep warm, remove the skewer. Put the walnuts in the pan from which you have just taken the bird, and fry them in the fat. Peel, core and thinly slice the apple, add it to the nuts and fry gently for a minute or two, then add the honey and vinegar, simmer gently until thoroughly cooked, season to taste and pour it, piping hot, over the bird. To serve, simply cut the bird in half. A very small portion of creamed potato could be served with this dish, and the salad must be eaten off a different plate.

The Salad

iceberg lettuce or Webb's Wonder
salt, sugar, pepper, lemon juice
¼ eating apple
2 oz/50 g walnut halves
2 tablespoons walnut oil

Plunge the lettuce into a bowl of iced water for a few minutes then drain it thoroughly. Place it in a salad bowl roughly broken up into manageable pieces and sprinkle with salt, sugar, pepper and lemon juice. Coarsely grate the apple and sprinkle it with lemon juice, then mix it in with the lettuce, toss in the walnuts and dribble the oil over. Serve very slightly chilled.

The English Treacle Tart

I chose treacle tart because when it is really well made and served with lemon soured cream it is so English and so delicious I feel sure Rossini would be delighted with it. This recipe is not quite traditional, as you will see. If you wish to use frozen short-crust pastry it is permissible so long as you are certain to serve the tart really well heated through.

For the pastry
4 oz/100 g plain flour
a pinch of salt
2½ oz/65 g unsalted butter
1 egg yolk
iced water as necessary

For the filling
2 oz/50 g ground hazelnuts
4 or 5 tablespoons of fresh white
*   breadcrumbs*
rind of ¼ lemon
6 tablespoons of golden syrup

Sift the flour with the salt added. Work the butter in with cold fingertips until it resembles breadcrumbs, then add the egg yolk beaten with a little water, adding more if needed until you have a smooth dough. Chill for 30 minutes. Line a greased 6 or 7 inch/15 or 17 centimetre flan tin, saving just a little of the pastry for decoration.

Mix the hazelnuts, finely grated lemon rind and breadcrumbs together and fill the pastry case. Warm the golden syrup and pour it all over the breadcrumb mixture. Roll out the remaining pastry and cut it into strips, lay it across the top of the tart to form a star-like pattern. Bake in a preheated oven 400°F/200°C/ Gas Mark 6 for 30 minutes approximately. Serve warm with a lightly whipped cream into which you have stirred a dessertspoon of lemon juice and a pinch of cinnamon.

York Ham in Port Grilled in a Field Mushroom

This savoury is quite delectable, and should be cooked at the very last moment, probably after a considerable pause.

*2 open field mushrooms (or
    cultivated ones will do if the field
    is not yielding just now)*
2 thin slivers of the finest York ham
2 tablespoons of port
1 oz/25 g butter
plenty of pepper
two pieces of toast

Place the mushrooms in a greased shallow flameproof dish. Cut the ham into thin strips and pile it into the mushrooms. Pour over the port, season with pepper and dot with butter. Grill under a fierce heat until it bubbles and colours slightly. Serve at once on the toast which you have cut into a round without crusts and very lightly buttered.

Index